Aristophanes: The *Clouds*

An Annotated Translation

Marie C. Marianetti

University Press of America, Inc.
Lanham • New York • London

Copyright © 1997 by
University Press of America,® Inc.
4720 Boston Way
Lanham, Maryland 20706

3 Henrietta Street
London, WC2E 8LU England

Library of Congress Cataloging-in-Publication Data

Aristophanes.
(Clouds. English)
The clouds : an annotated translation / Aristophanes ; (translated by)
Marie C. Marianetti.
p.   cm.
Includes bibliographical references.
1. Greek drama (Comedy)--Translations into English. I. Marianetti,
Marie C. II. Title.
PA 3877.N8 1996   882'.01--dc20   96-43480 CIP

ISBN 0-7618-0588-5 (pbk: alk. ppr.)

For Hannibal, my best and only friend
and for my mother, Eleni Tolou

Contents

Preface

The *Clouds* has been the most controversial and contradictory product of Aristophanes' genius. The play treats a multiplicity of subjects in such an intriguing and complicated manner that it has attracted the interest of many scholars and has generated an immense amount of scholarly literature.

There are numerous translations of the *Clouds* available and a diversity of secondary sources in circulation. My translation is an attempt to inform the general as well as the more specialized reader of what Aristophanes put on stage in 423 BC. I have tried to maintain a translation faithful to the original Greek, avoiding radical changes that would make the *Clouds* conform to linguistic "fads" at the very end of the twentieth century.

I have included the most important facts about the author and the play, and these are complemented by a chronological chart of the fifth century BC. and a selective bibliography for further reading. For this translation I have consulted Kenneth Dover's edition and Alan Sommerstein's translation of the *Clouds*.

Finally, my acknowledgments include everyone who kept encouraging me and helped me produce this book.

First and foremost I want to thank my Hannibal, whose affection and devotion kept inspiring me.

I wish to thank Professor Gary Schwartz of Lehman College for his help and support, friendship and encouragement, reading and suggestions.

I would like to express my special gratitude and appreciation to Professor David Bady of Lehman College for his patient and detailed reading of the manuscript, intelligent and valuable comments, contribution in organization and improvement of style, help in editing, and precious friendship.

Many thanks to Harry Fein for his assistance and advice.

This project was partly supported by a grant from The City University of New York/PSC-CUNY Research Award Program.

Marie C. Marianetti
Lehman College
The City University of New York
Bronx, New York
April 1996

Introduction

A. The Author

I. Life and Career

Aristophanes was born in Athens in the middle of fifth century BC. when Pericles was at the height of his power and Athens was the most powerful city-state in Greece.

The playwright's exact birthdate is in dispute; opinions vary from 452 to 444 BC. A native of the deme of Cydathenaeon, he was the son of an obscure middle-class figure named Philip and a very domineering woman named Zenodora.

In his lifetime, Aristophanes witnessed two radically different aspects of Athens' glory. He experienced the cultural, political, artistic, and intellectual developments during the Golden Age of Periclean democracy, with the works of Aeschylean tragedy which he admired and the revival of the poets of the past. He also saw the devastating results of the Peloponnesian War, the final destruction of Athenian glory, and the defeat of the city-state of Athens itself.

Most of his comedies were written during the Peloponnesian War, and in all of them Aristophanes offers contrasting views, comparing the devastating present to the brilliance of the past. His central theme is the welfare of the city-state of Athens. Since he is a conservative and traditionalist and an enemy of new ideas and movements, he criticizes all intellectuals as being a bad influence on the citizens and dislikes the sophists and the natural philosophers.

Aristophanes is a critic of the weaknesses of Athenian democracy, of radical social and economic theories, of demagogic leaders of the democratic party and of their imperialistic war policy. He displays an unsurpassed comic imagination and deals with contemporary issues through serious satire by exaggeration and caricature. He combines exquisite lyric poetry with obscenity, ribald jests, and vulgar farce.

The plots of Aristophanes are loosely constructed and his characters are generalized and subordinate to plot and humor. His style varies in simplicity and grace and his best known technique is his direct reference to real persons and events with slight allegory through the parabasis (the part of the play in which Aristophanes expresses his own voice and sentiments).

The Alexandrians knew of 44 plays by Aristophanes but we possess only 11 extant comedies. The following chronological chart sheds light on the key events that occurred in Athens during the Peloponnesian War, when Aristophanes was an active playwright, and it includes all extant plays of the author.

431	Outbreak of the Peloponnesian War
430	The Great Plague in Athens
429	Death of Pericles
428/7	Birth of Plato
427	Aristophanes' *Banqueters* (lost)
426	Aristophanes' *Babylonians* (lost)
425	Aristophanes' *Acharnians* (extant, won first prize at the Lenaia)
424	Aristophanes' *Knights* (extant, won first prize at the Lenaia)
423	Aristophanes' *Clouds* (extant but original lost, won third prize at the City Dionysia)
422	Aristophanes' *Wasps* (extant, won second prize at the Lenaia)
421	Peace Treaty between Sparta and Athens
	Aristophanes' *Peace* (extant, won second prize at the City Dionysia)
417?	Partial revision of Aristophanes' *Clouds* (extant but never performed)
415	Athens dispatches a great expedition to Sicily
414	Aristophanes' *Amphiaraos* (lost)
	Aristophanes' *Birds* (extant, won second prize at the City Dionysia)
413	Sparta resumes hostilities
	The Athenian expedition to Sicily is destroyed
411	Aristophanes' *Lysistrata* (extant, performed at the Lenaia)
	Aristophanes' *Thesmophoriazusai* (extant, performed at the City Dionysia)
	Oligarchic Revolution at Athens succeeds temporarily, but Democratic Constitution is restored some months later
408	Aristophanes' *Wealth* (lost)
406	Death of Euripides
	Death of Sophocles
405	Aristophanes' *Frogs* (extant, won first prize at the Lenaia)
	Defeat of Athens
404	Sparta imposes peace and an Oligarchic group, the Thirty Tyrants, put in power

II. Old/Political Comedy

Old Comedy is a term used to distinguish an earlier *genre* of Athenian comedy from the later Hellenistic dramatic form known as New Comedy. While New Comedy used stock characters reflecting realistic, living types (the courtesan, the slave, the miser, the adventurer, etc.) and a realistic plot, Old Comedy used a fantastic plot or a plot in which the reality of the situation was distorted in multiple ways to convey satiric criticism of the institutions, politicians, and war policies of the city-state of Athens.

Old Comedy, Aristophanes' own specialty, known also as Political Comedy, was closely associated with all aspects of the life of the *polis* (city-state) and was presented in publicly-supported festivals which were celebrated in honor of the multifaceted god Dionysos. Political Comedies were presented twice a year during the festivals of Lenaia and the Great, or City, Dionysia.

The festival of Lenaia[1] was celebrated during the Attic month *Gamelion* (January/February). Comic performances, at which dramatists and actors competed for excellence and received prizes, were first officially sponsored at the Lenaia of 440 BC.

The City Dionysia took place in the Attic month *Elaphebolion* (March/April). It was a pan-Hellenic festival; participants came from all over the Greek world. A religious procession carrying the statue of the god and the sacrifice of a bull began the festival. The City Dionysia, which lasted for three days, became the main place for dramatic competitions. The institution of comedy as an official part of the cult at the City Dionysia began around 486 BC.

The importance of the Great Dionysia reflected the importance of Dionysos himself, not only as the god of wine and joy but also as the god of vegetation and fertility, a representation of the birth-death-rebirth cycles of life. Dionysos is the god of life, reproduction, and fertility. The mythical story of his birth and rebirth[2] associates him with the cycle of the seasons and of the fertility of the earth.

Scholarship maintains that certain elements of Aristophanic comedy resemble elements of the earliest worship of the god Dionysos. They derive from the *comos*, a train of revelers very similar to a present day carnival, who paraded through town singing and dancing[3]. They wore masks and costumes so that no one would recognize them, and some wore or carried a huge *phallos*. All these processions were accompanied by singing, obscenity, raillery, and abuse directed toward individual members of the audience. Obscenity was the main feature. Clowns and jesters drove around in wagons and hurled obscenities at bystanders.

But obscenity and invective were parts of humor which had a ritualistic origin: they were means of driving away evil (an act known as *apotropaic*) and ensured good luck, especially in the realm of agricultural productivity and fertility. Often animals were also present in such processions, a fact which perhaps explains why the Aristophanic choruses often wore animal costumes. Thus the extensive satire and obscenity in Aristophanic comedy are derived from religious origins, and the comic play provides the same sacred release the wine and music of Dionysos did during the ritual celebration of the divinity.

A complementary scholarly assumption is that the term comedy might have originated from *come* (=village). Peasants came at night into the city and sang insulting songs outside the houses of citizens who had used them ill and taken advantage of them. In addition, in cases where peasants wanted favors from politicians or land owners, they would send out begging parties to ask for favors or express dissatisfaction, using obscenities and hiding their identities. Abuse, then, had a beneficial effect. The social benefits of such abuse were appreciated, and the peasants might have been told to repeat their performances in the theater concealing their identities with wine lees.

Evidence suggests that Sausarion from Megara (581-560) might have been the founder of comedy, or at least the institutor of comic plays.

III. *Production*

Comedies were performed in the theater of Dionysos located at the foot of the Acropolis in Athens. The theatrical apparatus consisted of the following features: (1) The circular dancing space in the middle known as the *orchestra*; (2) on the right and the left sides of the orchestra, the wings or *parodoi* which functioned as entrances and exits for the chorus (dancers) and the actors; (3) a rising auditorium for the audience that encircled half the orchestra; (4) the *skene*, located just behind the orchestra, where the actors changed their costumes. The skene was also used for the representation of various buildings, such as houses and palaces or even, through the use of painted scenery, of landscape. It had two or three doors, and a second level with windows and a roof, all of which were used for acting purposes.

Two mechanical devices also aided the production: the *mechane* and the *ekkyklema*. The *mechane*, a crane from which actors were suspended was used to create the illusion of flying gods and heroes. Hence the phrase more often used to describe tragic than comic episodes, *deus ex machina*. The *ekkyklema* was a wheeled platform which facilitated the display of "interior" scenes.

The number of plays to be performed at a festival was predetermined by officials who were appointed annually by lot to select the plays. Preparations for production began six months before the performance. The playwright could be the producer of his own plays or give them to someone else to produce, as Aristophanes often did.

The government provided each playwright with his chorus. The chorus of Old Comedy consisted of twenty-four member-dancers. The choruses of Aristophanic plays often portrayed animals, fish, or birds and were dressed in representational and very elaborate costumes with masks. They sang and danced as they moved their bodies. The provision and maintenance of costumes and the training of the chorus were undertaken by a special citizen known as *choregos*, who in Aristophanes' time was predominately a stage manager.

The actors were professionals and were employed and paid by the state. In Aristophanes' comedies the number of actors was generally three, although in some plays, like *Lysistrata,* a fourth actor was necessary. All actors were male and those who depicted male characters wore tights and a short *chiton* or tunic, with a huge erect or dangling *phallos* attached to their bodies. Actors who portrayed female roles wore a robe. Actors wore masks that portrayed their character or role. Real, living people were depicted by masks that were caricatures.

Each play lasted approximately two hours without an intermission. Old Comedies had the following structural features: (1) a *prologos* by the actors; (2) the *parodos* or entry of the chorus into the orchestra; (3) the *agon* or contest that took place between actors and chorus; (4) the *parabasis* or direct statement of the chorus or the chorus leader in the voice of the playwright to the audience; (5) various episodes acted by actors and odes sung by the chorus.

The plays were performed outdoors during the day. Night or darkness had to be indicated by use of a lamp or a torch. Because of its obscenity, Old Comedy was restricted to largely male audiences, although some women, slaves, and children may have been allowed to watch, seated or standing in the back of the theater. The front rows were reserved for government officials, foreign ambassadors, priests, and public figures.

Playwrights competed with one another and plays were awarded prizes determined by judges who were drawn by lot.

B. The Play

I. The Clouds *and Its Revisions*

The *Clouds* of Aristophanes was produced in 423 BC. at the festival of the City Dionysia. As was customary in an Athenian theatrical competition, Aristophanes competed with two other comedy playwrights, Kratinos, who won the first prize with his *Putine* (The Wine Flask), and Ameipsias, who won the second prize with his *Connus.* The *Clouds*, unfortunately, was placed third by the judges and this defeat hurt Aristophanes, who regarded the *Clouds* as one of the best and most intelligent of his plays (as is obvious from his comment in *Wasps* 1047).

There is scholarly evidence that Aristophanes subsequently revised the *Clouds*. Although the version of the play that we possess is not entirely different from the original, some parts have been added, others have been removed, new parts have been blended into previous parts and certain character exchanges have been rearranged. The major revisions of the play occur in three places:

(1) The parabasis (518-562), where Aristophanes talks bitterly about the failure of the original play and expresses his dissatisfaction to the audience and the judges, is evidently an addition to the original version.

(2) The contest between the Just and Unjust Arguments (889-1104) may have been substituted for an original discourse between Chaerephon and Pheidippides. In addition, a choral song containing cock-fighting imagery may have preceded the entry of the Just and Unjust Arguments in the original version.

(3) The burning of Socrates' Thinking Establishment belongs entirely to the revised version. We do not really know how the original version ended.

II. *The Plot*

The main character of the play is Strepsiades (=Mr. Twister), a very ambivalent, confused, and twisting character, who floats with the wind.

Strepsiades is a well-to-do peasant whose main income derives from the crops that his fields yield season after season. But he is married to a high-class Athenian woman from the well-known family of Megacles. She is a city woman who is spoiled by riches and comforts. Strepsiades and his wife have a son, Pheidippides, who takes after his maternal side and is encouraged to indulge in horse-racing and chariot-racing, both of which are expensive sports, requiring money for the purchase and maintenance of thoroughbred horses. Strepsiades is in debt because of his son's expensive habits, the product of his aristocratic breeding. He spends sleepless nights in figuring out how to avoid repaying his debts and cheat his creditors. He has heard of a new school of thought, the Thinking Establishment run by Socrates, which specializes in teaching forensic oratory to young men. Strepsiades, hoping that his son may learn how to argue on the wrong side and save him from his debts, tries to persuade Pheidippides to join Socrates' Thinking Establishment. But Pheidippides refuses, unwilling to lose his status and become the ridicule of his friends, the knights.

Strepsiades, then, in desperation, decides to join Socrates' school himself, despite his old age and state of forgetfulness. A student welcomes him and introduces him to the school's areas of specialization—cosmology, meteorology, geometry, and biology. The student attempts to impress Strepsiades by talking to him about Socrates' ingenuity and intelligence until Strepsiades at last meets the master himself, who makes an entrance suspended in a wicker basket in the air.

Socrates wants to know why Strepsiades wishes to attend his school and agrees to train him, provided that Strepsiades will adapt to the school's rules and requirements. The school, whose purpose is both rhetorical and scientific, also worships its own divinities. Entrance into Socrates' Thinking Establishment requires an initiation ceremony and reverence to different deities than the customary and traditional gods of the Greek pantheon. Strepsiades is introduced to the new Socratic gods: the Void, the Clouds, and the Tongue (each representing research and instruction at the school in the areas of natural phenomena and intellectual contemplation).

After Strepsiades is initiated, Socrates attempts to test his knowledge in metrical rhythms and grammatical refinement, but Strepsiades has neither proper knowledge of rhythms and grammar nor is he capable of absorbing appropriate instruction. Since he is too old for learning linguistic subtleties, he is advised to register his son, Pheidippides, instead.

Strepsiades, finally, succeeds in convincing Pheidippides to learn how to be able to twist a good argument and make the worse argument into the better. Father and son hear a debate between the Just and the Unjust Arguments. The Just praises the glorious culture, morality and education of earlier generations and contrasts them with the current decadent morals and values. The Unjust shows how intelligent speaking and training in oral discourse can open the doors to pleasures, security and success. Finally, father and son decide in favor of the Unjust, which possesses the power to make the weaker argument appear the stronger, in order to be able to evade their debts.

Pheidippides' education is completed, and father and son return home. Strepsiades, in his happiness and excitement, drives away two creditors who have come to collect their money. But even though everything seems perfect, Strepsiades and Pheidippides quarrel. They have dinner and Strepsiades asks Pheidippides to sing some old song. Pheidippides chooses a song by Euripides full of immoralities which infuriate Strepsiades. One argument leads to another and Pheidippides knocks his father down, an act grossly unacceptable to the traditional Greek culture. But Pheidippides, employing the Unjust Argument, proves to his father that he is right and that he would even be right to strike his own mother down.

Strepsiades regrets that he sent Pheidippides to learn the Unjust Argument and regrets his own decision to defraud his creditors and hoodwink the city. He realizes that he has been confused and misled by certain contemporary charlatans, and, in his anger, with the help of a servant sets fire to the Thinking Establishment and drives master Socrates and the students away.

III. *The Underlying Meaning of the* Clouds

The *Clouds* is a play about the social changes which became apparent in
Athens in mid-fifth century BC. It is not a play intended to attack Socrates
alone, or a play only about the sophistic revolution, or even a play only about
the pre-Socratic natural philosophers. The *Clouds* is a play about multiple themes,
different aspects and elements of the internal change that shook Athenian society
during a period of cultural disturbance. The basic characteristic of such a period
is the upsetting of cultural homeostasis in both the social and the individual
spheres. This is what the *Clouds* is about. Aristophanes' controversial plot,
multiple reversals, and variety of transformational roles underline his intention
to portray diverse forces opposed to one another in order to demonstrate the
changes that the Athenian state was experiencing and the impact that these
changes were having upon traditional citizens who still lived mindful of past
glories.

The *Clouds* of Aristophanes specifically reflects the Athenian state of mid-
fifth century in a process of cultural change by the diverse themes and the
variety of subjects which it explores. The generation gap between the two
characters, the father, Strepsiades, and the son, Pheidippides, is the culmination
of educational changes brought about by the sophistic revolution and natural
philosophy, movements that attempted to alter traditional beliefs and values by
the introduction of novelties unknown and confusing to the ordinary citizen.

At first, the philosopher Socrates seems to be the personal victim of
Aristophanic mockery. In reality, Socrates represents the play's main subject,
the sophistic corruption, and serves as the dramatist's scapegoat, through whom
the cultural polarities of Old and New, Tradition and Novelty, Peace and War,
Country and City, among others, are displayed. Aristophanes may have disliked
Socrates, but whether he actually considered Socrates a sophist we may never
know. Aristophanes' Socrates espouses a conglomeration of doctrines of various
individuals—Protagoras, Anaxagoras, Diagoras, Prodikos, Gorgias,
Thrasymachos—and the pre-Socratics in general.

The depiction of the Thinking Establishment as a religious institution relates
to certain religious cults (in particular the Orphic, Pythagorean, Bacchic,
Corybantic, Eleusinian, and that of Dionysos Sabazios), parodied by Aristophanes
in an attempt to show how atheism, scientific speculation, and the art of rhetorical
speaking were organized in a way similar to that of the older and more traditional
cults.

The *Clouds* as a play may then best be described as a reflection of the
conflict of opposites which it portrays. It emphasizes how a new ideology
regarding man and his environment confused the traditional ideas through which
man and his universe were viewed. Consequently, the play brings this diversity
together as the interplay of antithetical pairs of ideas which it exposes, and
which correspond to both conventional cultural traits and novel ideology. For
instance:

OLD (morality—Good)	*Vs*	**NEW** (amorality—Bad)
Tradition (gods, festivals rituals, rites)	*Vs*	**Novelty** (intellectual contemplation, skepticism, materialism)
Country life (Strepsiades before his marriage)	*Vs*	**City life** (Strepsiades' wife, Pheidippides)
Lower class (peasantry)	*Vs*	**Upper class** (aristocracy)
Agriculture (farming)	*Vs*	**Political** skills and training in the law courts
Outdoor life (good health, physical strength)	*Vs*	**Indoor** life (pallor, sickly complexion, Socrates' school)
Hard physical work	*Vs*	**Idleness** and up-in-the-air nebulosities
Physical exercise (performed outdoors)	*Vs*	**Mental** exercise (performed indoors)
Peasant rascality and vulgarism	*Vs*	**Sophistic** intricacy and deception
Cloud-Chorus (associated with tradition and nature)	*Vs*	**Cloud-Chorus** (representing the Socratic deities)

Finally, the oppositional and double role of the Clouds both as traditional moralizers and as novel divinities, embodies all the binary oppositions of the play, and epitomizes the conflicts which brought confusion to conventional citizens, and functioned as agents of the cultural change that took place in mid-fifth century Athens.

Notes

1   Lenaia is derived from *lene*, which signifies "maenad." Maenads, Bacchae, or Thyiades were mythological female followers of Dionysos, inspired to ecstatic frenzy in honor of the god. They were known to wear fawn or panther skins and wreaths of ivy, oak, or fir, and to carry snakes, wave wands or torches, and celebrate the power of Dionysos in song, music, and dance. They roamed through mountains and woods oblivious of all human concerns, conventions, and fears. Dionysos inspired them with strength so that they could uproot trees and kill strong animals. They hunted animals and ate their raw flesh, believing that they thereby received the body and blood of Dionysos, in a ritualistic act known as *omophagy* (the eating of raw flesh) a rite equivalent to the holy communion of Christianity.

2   There are different mythological accounts of Dionysos' birth. The most explicit representation of the religious concept of birth-death-rebirth is the one adopted by the Orphics: Zeus mated with his daughter Persephone and bore Dionysos, nicknamed Zagreos. Hera in her jealousy sent the Titans to attack the child. The Titans, having disguised themselves with white powder, found and dismembered the baby Dionysos. Athena recovered Dionysos' heart, and took it to Zeus, who swallowed it. Dionysos was reborn, this time begotten of Zeus and Semele. The Titans were destroyed by Zeus with lightning and thunder, and from their ashes mankind is born—associated with their evil. Thus Dionysos represents the force of good, the mystery of reproduction and fertility, and nature itself.

3   The following categories of revelers were the usual followers of god Dionysos: (1) *ithyphalloi* were the followers of Dionysos carrying the *phallos*; (2) *phallophoroi* were garlanded with leaves and flowers and were led by a youth with soot-blackened face wearing the *phallos*; (3) *autokabdaloi* were buffoon improvisers.

Characters of the Play

Strepsiades of Cicynna, son of Pheidon

Pheidippides, a playboy, son of Strepsiades

Xanthias, slave of Strepsiades

Student of Socrates

Socrates, the stereotypical philosopher

Koryphaios or Chorus Leader

Tradition (the Better or Just Argument)

Novelty (the Worse or Unjust Argument)

Pasias, first creditor of Strepsiades

Amynias, second creditor of Strepsiades

Chaerephon, student of Socrates

[It's night. Strepsiades and his son Pheidippides are asleep. Strepsiades, who dreams of his debts, is restless; he wakes up and talks to himself]

STREPSIADES

Woe is me, woe is me!
Oh Zeus, lord, what a length of nighttime.
It's endless. Won't it ever be daytime?
But I heard a rooster crow a long time ago.
And the slaves are snoring. But they wouldn't
have gotten away with it in the old good days.   5
Damn you war, damn you on many accounts,
when it's not even possible for me to punish my slaves.[1]
But not even this good young fellow here
wakes up before the daylight; he is just farting away
covered in five fleeced blankets.   10
All right, if it seems right to you, let's snore under the covers.
[Strepsiades tries to go back to sleep but he can't]
But I can't sleep, wretched me, being bitten
by expenses and stable-fees and debts
because of this son of mine. And he wears his hair long[2]
and rides horses and pairs of chariots   15
and dreams of horses. And I perish
when I see the moon in its twenties[3]
for the interest piles up.
[Strepsiades calls for his slave Xanthias]
                        Hey boy, light a lamp
and fetch my accounts, so that I can see
how many creditors I owe and calculate the interest.   20
[The slave wakes up and brings the accounts to Strepsiades]
Bring them, let me see, what do I owe? Twelve minas[4] to Pasias.
Twelve minas to Pasias? What did I use them for?
Oh yes, when I bought the *koppa*-branded horse.[5] Oh wretched me,
I wish I had first knocked my eye out with a stone.

PHEIDIPPIDES *[He dreams and talks in his sleep]*

Pheilon, you are cheating. Drive in your own lane.   25

STREPSIADES

This is the very evil that has ruined me;
for he sleeps and dreams of racing horses.

PHEIDIPPIDES [*Asleep*]

How many laps will the war chariots drive?

STREPSIADES

You are driving me, your father, many laps.
Yet, what debt befell me after Pasias?   30
Three minas to Amynias for a chariot board and wheels.

PHEIDIPPIDES [*Still asleep*]

Let the horse roll around and then take him to the stable.

STREPSIADES

But, sweetie, you have rolled me out of my house,
when I have lost lawsuits and the other creditors
are saying that they will confiscate for their interest.

PHEIDIPPIDES [*Wakes up*]

                              Really, father, why have   35
you been distressed and tossing around all night long?

STREPSIADES

Some deme official[6] in the mattress bites me.

PHEIDIPPIDES

Oh wretched you, let me sleep for a while.

STREPSIADES

All right, you sleep then. But know that these debts
will all turn on your head.   40
Alas!
May the matchmaker who urged me
to marry your mother drop dead.
For life was rustic and very sweet to me,
lying around purposelessly, unwashed, insatiate,
surrounded by bees, sheep and pressed olives.   45
And then I married the niece of Megacles, son of Megacles,[7]

I a farmer, she from the city,
an arrogant, voluptuous, *Koesyrated grande dame*.[8]
When I married her, I lay in bed
smelling of wine, figs, wool and riches,   50
and she of perfume, saffron, tonguekisses,
extravagance, gluttony, Kolias and Genetyllis.[9]
And I wouldn't say that she was slow, but she weaved,
and I would tell her jokingly, showing her this
very cloak: "Hey, woman, you weave too much."[10]   55

[*The lamp light goes out*]

XANTHIAS

We have no more oil in the lamp.

STREPSIADES

Damn it. Why did you light me the thirsty lamp?
Come here so that you may weep.

XANTHIAS

                                            And why shall I weep?

STREPSIADES

Because you put in one of the fat wicks.
[*The slave leaves and Strepsiades continues his monologue*]
After these things, when this son was born to us,   60
to me, in fact, and my good wife,
then we fought about his name.
She wanted to add *hippos*[11] to his name,
like "Xanthippos," or "Charippos," or even "Calippides,"
but I wanted to name him Pheidonides[12] after his grandfather.   65
Meanwhile we disputed, and then with time
we came to an agreement and named him Pheidippides.[13]
She used to hold this son and fondle him:
"When you grow up and drive the chariot to the city,
like Megacles, wearing your distinguished robe—"And I would say: 70
"When you drive the goats from the rocklands,
just like your father, dressed in a leather cloak—"
He did not listen to any of my words,
but wasted my property with his horse-mania.

And now, trying to figure out a way all night long,   75
I have found an extraordinary heaven-sent pathway,
with which I'll be saved if I persuade my son here.
But first I want to wake him up.
What would be the sweetest way to wake him up? How?
[*He calls Pheidippides*]
Pheidippides, my little Pheidippides!

PHEIDIPPIDES

What is it father?   80

STREPSIADES

Kiss me and give me your right hand.[14]

PHEIDIPPIDES   [*Gets up and gives his right hand to Strepsiades*]

Here it is. What is it?

STREPSIADES

Tell me, do you love me?

PHEIDIPPIDES

Yes, by Poseidon, the very Lord of horses.

STREPSIADES

No, no to this Lord of horses.
For this god is responsible for my misfortunes.   85
But if you love me from your heart indeed,
obey me, my son.

PHEIDIPPIDES

In what way shall I obey you?

STREPSIADES

Change your way of life as fast as possible
and go to learn the things I tell you to.

PHEIDIPPIDES

Tell me, what do you bid me?

STREPSIADES

Will you obey?

PHEIDIPPIDES

I will obey,   90
in the name of Dionysos.

STREPSIADES

Now look over here.
Do you see that little door and the little house?

PHEIDIPPIDES

I see them. But what is it really, father?

STREPSIADES

This is the Thinking Establishment[15] for wise spirits.
There live men who mesmerize us by saying how   95
the sky is like an oven,
and it's all over us, and we are the charcoals.
These people teach, if someone gives them money,
how to win talking both honestly and dishonestly.[16]

PHEIDIPPIDES

Who are they?

STREPSIADES

I don't exactly know their name.   100
But they are anxious thinkers, good and fine fellows.

PHEIDIPPIDES

Oh, I know, the rotten ones. You are talking about the
charlatans, the palefaces, the fellows without shoes,
among whom are the god-hated Socrates and Chaerephon.

STREPSIADES

Oh, be quiet. Don't say anything childish.   105
But if you care for your father's daily food,
become one of them and abandon horse racing.

PHEIDIPPIDES

No way, in the name of Dionysos, not even if you gave me
the pheasants that Leogoras raises.[17]

STREPSIADES

Come on, I implore you, dearest of people to me,   110
go there and learn.

PHEIDIPPIDES

                              And what shall I learn for you?

STREPSIADES

They say that there are among them two arguments,[18]
the better, whatever this may be, and the worse.
And that one among this pair of arguments, the worse,
they say that it wins arguing on the wrong side.   115
So if you learn this unjust argument for me,
then on all those debts that I owe because of you
I won't have to pay back even an obol to anyone.

PHEIDIPPIDES

I won't listen to you; I wouldn't even dare look
at the knights with all color faded from my face.   120

STREPSIADES

Then, by Demeter, you will not eat anything of mine—
neither you, nor your horse, not even your *San*-branded
breed. I'll throw you out of the house—To hell with you.

PHEIDIPPIDES

But uncle Megacles won't leave me without a horse.
I am leaving and I do not care about you.   125
[*Pheidippides goes into the house*]

STREPSIADES

And I will not take this blow lying down,
but with a prayer to the gods, I myself will get taught,
going to the Thinking Establishment.
But then how shall I learn quibbling arguments
being an old man, forgetful and slow?   130
I must go. Why am I twisting myself with these thoughts
and not knocking at the door?
[*He knocks at the door of the Thinking Establishment*]
                                    Hey boy, little boy.

STUDENT [*From inside*]

Go to hell. Who is knocking at the door?
[*The student opens the door*]

STREPSIADES

Strepsiades the son of Pheidon from the deme of Cicynna.

STUDENT

In the name of Zeus, you are ignorant, whoever you are   135
who has kicked the door so hard and thoughtlessly
and destroyed an idea that was being born.

STREPSIADES

I am sorry. I'm only a country bumpkin.
But tell me about the idea that miscarried.

STUDENT

But it is not permitted to tell any one except the students.[19]   140

STREPSIADES

Tell me with courage for I have come as a student
to this very Thinking Establishment.

STUDENT

I shall tell you. But you must consider these holy secrets.
Sometime ago, Socrates asked Chaerephon
how far—in flea-feet—a flea can jump,   145
because one had bitten the eyebrow of Chaerephon
and jumped onto the head of Socrates.

STREPSIADES

And then how did he measure it out?

STUDENT

                              Very artistically.
He melted wax and then took the flea
and dipped in the wax both its feet, around   150
which, when the wax became cold, Persian boots grew.[20]
He took these off and measured the distance.

STREPSIADES

Oh Zeus, Lord, what mental refinement!

STUDENT

Would you like to hear another idea
of Socrates?

STREPSIADES

                    Which one? I beg you, tell me.   155

STUDENT

> Chaerephon of Sphettos asked him
> the opinion that he held as to whether gnats
> tootled through their mouths or through their butts.

STREPSIADES

> And what did he say about the gnat?

STUDENT

> He said that the intestine of the gnat   160
> is narrow, and that the air is forced through
> this fine tube straight to the rump.
> And then, being a cavity at the end of the narrow passage,
> the asshole farts by the force of the wind.

STREPSIADES

> Therefore the asshole is the trumpet of the gnats.   165
> Oh thrice blessed the farter amongst mortals!
> It would be very easy for someone who knows
> the intestinal tract of the gnats to escape a trial.

STUDENT

> And the other day he was distracted from a great
> discovery because of a spotted lizard.

STREPSIADES

>   In what way? Tell me.   170

STUDENT

> While he was investigating the paths and the revolutions
> of the moon, and he was gazing opened-mouthed at the sky,
> a spotted lizard shit on him from the roof in the dark.

STREPSIADES [*Amused*]

> I am glad that the lizard shit all over Socrates.

STUDENT

Yesterday evening there was no dinner for us.   175

STREPSIADES

And how did he manage to get your daily food?

STUDENT

After he sprinkled on the table a fine film of ashes,
he bent a skewer and then having made a compass,
he hooked a cloak from the wrestling place.

STREPSIADES

Why then do we admire Thales?[21]   180
Then open, open the Thinking Establishment
and show me Socrates as fast as possible.
I want to learn. Open the door.
[*Strepsiades sees pale-faced students and is surprised*]
Oh Heracles, where did these monsters come from?

STUDENT

Why do you look astonished? What do they look like?   185

STREPSIADES

Like the Laconians, the men who were captured at Pylos.
But why do they stare at the ground?

STUDENT

They are searching for things that are on the earth.

STREPSIADES

                            So they are searching for bulbs.
Do not even think about it again.
For I know where the good and big ones are.   190
[*Strepsiades points to another group of students*]
And what are these men who are bending so much doing?

STUDENT

They are searching into darkness below Tartaros.[22]

STREPSIADES

And why do their assholes look toward the sky?

STUDENT

They teach themselves astronomy.
[*Talks to the other students*]
Go inside so that he may not see you here.   195

STREPSIADES

Not yet, not yet, let them stay, so that
I can inform them about my problem.

STUDENT

They cannot spend so much time outside
in the air.
[*The students go inside*]

STREPSIADES [*Astonished at some hanging instruments*]

For heaven's sake, what are these things? Tell me.   200

STUDENT

This is for Astronomy.

STREPSIADES

                                        And what is this for?

STUDENT

Geometry.

STREPSIADES

                                        And what is this used for?

STUDENT

To measure land.

STREPSIADES

The land allotted to the clerurchs?[23]

STUDENT

No, the entire earth.

STREPSIADES

You are joking.
The device is useful and democratic.   205

STUDENT

And this is the map of the entire world. Do you see it?
And here is Athens.

STREPSIADES

What are you saying? I do not believe you,
since I do not see any jurors on their benches.

STUDENT

Truly, this is the land of Attica.

STREPSIADES

And where are my demesmen, the men from Cicynna?   210

STUDENT

They are here. And this is Euboea, as you see,
which stretches for a very long way.

STREPSIADES

I know, because it was stretched out by us and Pericles.[24]
But where is Lacedaemon?

STUDENT [*Points toward Sparta*]

        Where is it? Here it is.

STREPSIADES

 How close to us. Figure out a way   215
 to move it a long way away from us.

STUDENT

 But this cannot be.

STREPSIADES

      In the name of Zeus, you're going to shout.
[*He looks up and sees Socrates hanging from a basket*]
 Come, who is this man in the hanger?

STUDENT

 He, Himself.[25]

STREPSIADES

     Himself, Who?

STUDENT

       Socrates.

STREPSIADES

       Oh Socrates!
 Come, you, call out to him for me loudly.   220

STUDENT

 You call him yourself; I have no time to spare.

STREPSIADES

 Socrates!
 Little Socrates!

SOCRATES

Why are you calling me, creature of the day?

STREPSIADES

First, tell me what you are doing, I implore you.

SOCRATES

I walk on the air and I speculate about the sun. 225

STREPSIADES

Then, why do you look down upon the gods from the basket
and not from the ground, if at all?

SOCRATES

I would never
find out about the celestial phenomena[26]
unless I hang up my mind, and mixed my
rare thought with the air that it resembles. If I were 230
on the ground and investigated the things above from below,
I would never discover anything, because the earth
pulls toward itself the moisture of thought by force.
And the same thing happens to the cress.

STREPSIADES [*Perplexed*]

What are you saying? 235
The thought draws moisture to the cress?
Come now, little Socrates, come down to me
in order that you may teach me those things for which I came.

SOCRATES [*Descends to the ground*]

What did you come for?

STREPSIADES

Wishing to learn the art of speaking,
because I am plundered and swept away by some 240
very harassing creditors, and I have pledged my property.

SOCRATES

How did you come in debt without noticing it?

STREPSIADES

A horse epidemic destroyed me and ate me up terribly.
But teach me one of your two arguments,
the one that evades repayment. And whatever fee   245
you may charge me, I swear to gods that I will give it to you.

SOCRATES

To what gods do you swear? First of all we
do not credit any gods.

STREPSIADES

                              By what do you swear then?
By the iron coins, just as those people in Byzantion?

SOCRATES

Do you want to know accurately about the divine things   250
as they are truly?

STREPSIADES

                              By Zeus, if it's possible.

SOCRATES

And to communicate in conversation with the Clouds,
who are our deities?

STREPSIADES

                              Very much so.

SOCRATES

Then sit on this sacred couch.[27]

STREPSIADES

Look, I am sitting.

SOCRATES

Then take this garland.   255

STREPSIADES

What garland? Wretched me, Socrates,
do not sacrifice me like Athamas.[28]

SOCRATES

No, but we do all these things to people who are going to be
initiated.

STREPSIADES

Then what shall I gain?

SOCRATES

You'll become a fluent talker, a cymbal, a fine flour of   260
dishonesty. Don't get shook up!

[*Socrates sprinkles Strepsiades with fine flour*]

STREPSIADES

By Zeus, you aren't lying to me,
because I am being sprinkled and floured.

SOCRATES

It is necessary that I speak; listen to the prayer.
Oh Lord, god, immeasurable Air, you who hold the earth suspended,
and shining Aether, and you solemn lightning-thundered Cloud
    Goddesses,   265
arise, oh maidens, appear to the thinker suspended on the air.

STREPSIADES [*Tries to cover up with his cloak*]

Not yet, not before I wrap myself in this, so that I do not get wet.
What demon possessed me to come from home without a cap?

SOCRATES

Come then, oh majestic Clouds, to display yourselves to this man.
Whether you sit on the snowy, holy peaks of Olympos
or you are engaged in a holy dance with the Nymphs in   270
    the garden of your father, Ocean,
whether you draw water from the golden mouth of the Nile
or you occupy lake Maeotis or the snowy rock of Mimas,
listen, accept the sacrifice and rejoice in the holy rites.

CHORUS

Eternal Clouds,   275
let us appear in our radiant, dewy form
departing from deep-roaring father Ocean
    to the peaks of high-standing mountains
    full of trees, so that   280
    we may see the peaks showing from far away
    and the sacred earth whose crops we water
    and the flow of the divine rivers
    and the deep-thundering flowing sea;
    for the eye of heaven beams brightly tireless   285
with sparkling rays.
But shaking off the rainy mist
    from our immortal forms, let us look
    upon the earth with far-seeing eye.   290

SOCRATES

Oh most solemn Clouds, you clearly listened to me when I called you.
[*He turns to Strepsiades*]
Did you hear their voice together with the roar of the divine thunder?

STREPSIADES

Indeed, and I revere you, oh my honored ones, and I wish
    to fart back as an
answer to the thunder. How scared I am by them and shaken up.
And whether it's allowed, or not, I will crap.   295

SOCRATES

Do not joke anymore and stop doing those things that the comedians do,
but speak up because a great swarm of goddesses moves on with songs.

CHORUS

Rain-bearing maidens,
let us go to the sunny land of Pallas Athena,[29] and see   300
the lovely land of Kekrops,[30] home of fine men.
   where there is reverence of the rites not to be spoken of,
   where the house of the Mysteries
   is opened at the holy festivities;
   where there is gift-giving to the heavenly gods   305
   and where there are high-standing temples and statues,
   and very holy processions to the blessed ones
   and garlanded sacrifices to the gods
at every season,   310
the Dionysian delight with the coming spring
   and the excitement of the well-sung dances
   and the deep-sounding music of the pipe.

STREPSIADES

By Zeus, I implore you, tell me, Socrates, who are these
   women
who are singing this holy song; are they some heroines?   315

SOCRATES

Not at all, they are the heavenly Clouds, great goddesses
   among lazy men,
who bestow on us judgment and discourse and intelligence,
manipulation, circumlocution, deception and assault.

STREPSIADES

That is why my soul has taken wing after hearing their voices
and already desires to talk finely and quibble about smoke,   320
pricking one judgment with a little judgment of my own and
   argument with counter-argument.
Therefore, if it's possible, I wish now to see them clearly.

The Clouds

SOCRATES

Now look here toward Mt. Parnis, for I see them
coming down quietly.

STREPSIADES

Where are they? Show me.

SOCRATES

A great many of them are coming through
the valleys and the forests; they are at your side.   325

STREPSIADES [*Looking at the sky*]

What is wrong?
I can't see them.

SOCRATES

In the wing-entrance.

STREPSIADES

I just now see them.

[*The Clouds enter in the shape of women*]

SOCRATES

Now you see them, indeed, unless you have pumpkins for eyes.

STREPSIADES

By Zeus, I do. Oh venerable Ladies. They take up the entire space.

SOCRATES

And you did not know or believe that they were goddesses?

STREPSIADES

In the name of Zeus, I thought that they were mist, dew,
and smoke.   330

SOCRATES

For you don't know, by Zeus, that these nourish many
    wise men,
diviners from Thurii, men of the medical art, and men with
long hair flopping with rings and natty nails, song composers
    for circular dances, men of airy quackery;
they sustain idle men who do nothing, just because they sing
    poetry for them.

STREPSIADES

That is why they write about the "dreadful whirling of the
    rain-bearing clouds with bright rage,"   335
and the "locks of the hundred-headed Typhoeus"[31] and the
    "hard-blowing storms,"
and then the "aerial birds floating on the air," and "crook-
    taloned birds floating on the air," and
"rains of waters from the dewy clouds;" then to compensate
    themselves for this, they swallow
slices of the beautiful big fish and the avian flesh of
    thrushes.

SOCRATES

And all these things because of the Clouds. Isn't it just?   340

STREPSIADES

                        Then tell me, if they are indeed
clouds, what must have they undergone to make them look like
mortal women? For those clouds up there are not like these.

SOCRATES

                        Tell me what do they look like?

STREPSIADES

I do not know exactly. They look like flocks of spread out wool,
not like women, but, by Zeus, these have noses.

SOCRATES

Now answer these things that I ask you.   345

STREPSIADES

Tell me whatever you want as fast as you can.

SOCRATES

Have you ever looked up and seen a cloud resembling a
centaur or a leopard or a wolf or even a bull?

STREPSIADES

Oh yes, in the name of Zeus. So what about it?

SOCRATES

They become everything that they wish, and if they see a
long-haired savage, of these shaggy men, just like the son of Xenophantes,[32]
they joke with his passion by resembling centaurs.[33]   350

STREPSIADES

And what do they do if they see a plunderer of the public
    treasury like Simon?[34]

SOCRATES

They reveal his nature by turning into wolves.

STREPSIADES

That is why, after they saw Kleonymos[35] the shield-dropper
    yesterday,
they became deer, because they saw him as a coward.

SOCRATES

And now they have seen Kleisthenes,[36] as you see,   355
    and for this reason they have turned into women.

STREPSIADES

Hail, oh maidens; and now, if you've done so for someone else,
utter a sky long sound for me too, heavenly ones.

CHORUS

Hail, oh old man, born in the old times, hunter of poetic arguments.
[*To Socrates*]
And you, priest of fine utterances, tell us what you need
because we won't listen to anyone else among the present day
    celestial thinkers,   360
but only to Prodicos,[37] him because of his wisdom and judgment,
and you because you swagger barefooted in the streets and you roll
your eyes and endure many misfortunes and assume a solemn
    countenance because of us.

STREPSIADES

Oh earth, what a sound! How holy, and divine and portentous!

SOCRATES

For these are the only goddesses; everything else is just nonsense.   365

STREPSIADES

Come on, in the name of the earth, wouldn't you consider Olympian
    Zeus a god?

SOCRATES

Zeus who? Don't speak nonsense. There isn't any Zeus.

STREPSIADES

                        What are you talking about?
But who causes the rain? Answer me this first of all.

SOCRATES

These clouds do. And I will demonstrate it to you with strong evidence.
Come on, where have you ever seen it rain without the clouds?   370
Although it is expected that Zeus should be able to make rain from
    a clear sky, when they are away.

STREPSIADES

By Apollo, what you say supports what you were saying.
Although before I thought that Zeus was pissing from the sieve.
But tell me, who makes the thunder, who is the one who makes
    me tremble?

SOCRATES

These produce the thunder when they roll over.   375

STREPSIADES

                                In which way, oh you daring one?

SOCRATES

When they are filled with water and need to move,
hanging full of rain and heavy, they fall against one
another breaking loose and crashing.

STREPSIADES

But isn't it Zeus who makes them move by necessity?

SOCRATES

No, it's the celestial vortex.[38]

STREPSIADES

                        The celestial vortex? I forgot that Zeus   380
no longer exists and that in his place now rules vortex.
But you have not taught me anything yet about the crash
    and the thunder.

SOCRATES

Didn't you hear me saying that when the clouds are full of
water they fall at one another and crash because of their density?

STREPSIADES

Come on, who is going to believe that?   385

SOCRATES

I will teach you from your own body.
Have you ever filled yourself with soup from the Panathenaean festival[39]
and then were disturbed in your stomach when a fart rumbled through it?

STREPSIADES

Yes, by Apollo, and it harmed me and shook me right away,
and, just like thunder crashes, the little soup makes a fearful noise,
first gently papapax, papapapax and then comes
    papapapapapaaaaxxx!   390
and when I shit, it thunders papapapaaaxx, exactly like they do.

SOCRATES

Now just think how much you can fart from this little stomach.
And this air that is endless, how loudly would it be likely to
    thunder?
That is why the names for *bronte* [thunder] and
    porde [fart] sound alike.

STREPSIADES

But show me where the lightning shining with fire
    comes from,   395
which burns us alive when it strikes us.
For clearly Zeus sends this against the perjurers.

SOCRATES

And how come, oh you stupid idiot, smelling of the age
    of Kronos,[40] lunatic man,
if he punishes the perjurers, he did not punish Simon
or Kleonymos or even Theoros[41] although they are
    exceedingly perjurers?   400
But instead he strikes his own temple and Sunion,[42] the edge of Athens,
and the large oak trees,[43] wishing to find out what? For the
    oak tree cannot be a perjurer.

STREPSIADES

I do not know; but it seems that you speak well. What is then
    the thunderbolt?

SOCRATES

When a dry wind rises in the air and gets shut inside the clouds,
from the inside it then blows them up like a bladder, and then
    by necessity   405
it bursts them and comes out heavy because of its density
and by the whistling and rush it burns itself out.

STREPSIADES

By Zeus, and I suffered the same ignorantly sometime ago at the Diasia.[44]
I was roasting a paunch filled with minced meat for my relatives and
    forgot to slit it,
and it started blowing up and all of the sudden it exploded   410
and befouled my eye with dung and burned my face.

CHORUS

Oh man, you who desire a great wisdom from us,
how happy you will become among the Athenians and the Greeks
if you have good memory and are a good thinker and you endure hardship
in the soul, and you do not get tired whether standing or walking   415
and you neither grieve too much for being cold nor do you desire breakfast
and you abstain from wine and exercises and all other stupidities
and you consider this the best, which befits a clever man—
to win in action and deliberation, fighting with the tongue.

STREPSIADES

Don't worry about my ability to endure a hard bed   420
and an ill-fed, worn-out stomach—I am confident about these
and I would hand in myself to mold to your purpose.

SOCRATES

Then you will not credit any other god except those that we do,
the Chaos, and the Clouds and the Tongue—these three?[45]

STREPSIADES

I wouldn't even talk to the other gods if I met them, nor
    would I answer them,   425
and I wouldn't sacrifice to them or pour libations or even put
    incense on their altars.

CHORUS

With confidence, tell us now what we can do for you,
    since you'll not be unlucky
to honor us and respect us and seek to be a clever man.

STREPSIADES

Oh maidens, I ask you this very small thing—that I may be
the best among the Greeks in the art of speaking for miles and miles. 430

CHORUS

This will be yours from us, so that from now on,
no one in the public arena will carry more motions than you.

STREPSIADES

Do not talk to me about great motions, for I do not desire them,
but only to twist justice for myself and evade my creditors.

CHORUS

You will gain those things that you yearn for; for you do not
    desire impossible things.   435
But hand yourself over with confidence to our priests.

STREPSIADES

I shall do these things, trusting you; for necessity presses me
because of the *koppa*-branded horses and the wedding that
    ruined me.
So now, as they wish, I will give my
body to them to be beaten   440
to hunger, to thirst, to be dirty,
to be cold, to be thrashed into a wineskin,
if I can escape my debts.
I will show the people that I am
bold, eloquent, daring, reckless,   445
loathsome, a shameless liar,
fluent, a pettifogger,
a lawyer, a cymbal, a fox, a needle's eye,
a thong, a dissembler, a knavish, an arrogant customer

marked with a sting, a villain, a twister, troublesome,   450
a meal devourer.
And if they make those who meet me call me these things,
they can do anything that they want;
and if they wish,
by Demeter, they can make a gut string of me   455
and give it to the thinking students.

CHORUS

This man has spirit,
    he is not a coward, he is ready.
Know that
    when you learn these things from me you will have   460
a glory stretching to the sky among the mortals.

STREPSIADES

What shall I suffer?

CHORUS

                          All the time with me
you will have the most
    envied life of men.   465

STREPSIADES

Will I ever
    see this?

CHORUS

                               Yes, so that
many people will always
    sit by your threshold,
wishing to consult you and talk with you   470
    about indictments and affairs worth
many talents
    valuing your mind,
while they are taking your advice.   475

[*To Socrates*]
    Give the old man whatever you are to teach him preliminarily,
    and stir up his mind and test his intelligence.

SOCRATES

Come on now, tell me about your behavior
so that, knowing what it is, I can attack it,
with the newest devices.   480

STREPSIADES

What then? For heaven's sake, do you think of besieging me?

SOCRATES

No, but I want to learn a few things from you.
For instance, do you have a good memory?

STREPSIADES

                                It works two ways, by Zeus.
If something is owed to me, I remember very well,
and if I, the wretched one, owe, I am very forgetful.   485

SOCRATES

Is then for you the talent of speech natural?

STREPSIADES

Not for speaking, but for evading.

SOCRATES

So how are you going to be able to learn?

STREPSIADES

                            Very well, don't worry about it.

SOCRATES

Come on now: whenever I throw you something wise
about natural phenomena, you must grasp it right away.   490

STREPSIADES

What? Will I feed myself with wisdom like a dog?

SOCRATES

This man is ignorant and a barbarian.
I fear, old man, that you need the rod.
Come on, let me see, what do you do if someone strikes you?

STREPSIADES

                                        I get hit,
and then after waiting for a little bit I call on witnesses;   495
and then after waiting for very short time I go to the law.

SOCRATES

Come on, now, take your cloak off.

STREPSIADES

                              Did I do anything wrong?

SOCRATES

No, but it's believed that you should enter naked.

STREPSIADES

No, but I'm not searching for a thief!

SOCRATES

Take it off. What are you talking about?

STREPSIADES

                              Tell me this now: 500
If I am disciplined and learn willingly,
which of your students will I look like?

SOCRATES

You will not differ in nature from Chaerephon.

STREPSIADES

Oh, wretched me, I will be half dead.

SOCRATES

No, you should not talk but hurry up and follow me   505
here quickly.

STREPSIADES

But before anything else
give me a honey sweet in my hand. I am scared to descend
as though into the cave of Trophonios.[46]

SOCRATES

Move on. What do you keep hanging around the door for?

CHORUS

But go rejoicing   510
because of this courage.

May happiness befall
     the man, because advancing
deeply into old age
he dyes himself with newer   515
     things than his nature
and pursues knowledge.

CHORUS LEADER

Oh spectators, I[47] shall tell you freely
the truth, by Dionysos who has nourished me.
So may I win and may I be considered wise   520
as I believed that you were clever spectators
and that this is the wisest of my comedies,

I honored you to have a taste of it first, the one that has
cost me the most labor; then I departed, defeated by vulgar
men not deserving victory. So I blame you among the   525
intelligent people, for whose sake I got into trouble.
But I will never betray willingly the clever ones among you.
For since the time when in this place my virtuous fellow and
my vicious fellow[48] were well spoken of by certain men
       whom it is a pleasure to mention,
and I, for I was still a virgin and somehow not supposed to
       give birth,   530
exposed it, and someone else took the child and raised it,
[To spectators]
       and you reared it and educated it generously,
       and from that time I have sworn faith to your judgment.
So now this comedy has come like Electra,[49]
seeking to find intelligent spectators somewhere.   535
For she recognizes the lock of her brother's hair, when she sees it.
Look how modest she is by disposition, she who first
did not come stitched with a dangling leather,
red at the end, and fat, so that would be laughter among the children;
nor did she scold the bald men, nor danced she a cordax;[50]   540
Nor does the old man with the leading role hit any one
who is present with his stick, hiding his sense of wit.
Nor did this comedy enter holding torches or did it cry aloud "iou," "iou;"
but it has come trusting in itself and the plot;
and I myself being the poet don't wear my hair long,[51]   545
nor do I present the same thing twice and thrice in order to cheat you,
but I always devise to introduce new ideas
no one the same as the other and all of them clever;
I, who hit Kleon in the stomach when he was a demagogue,[52]
and I did not dare jump on him once more when he was down.   550
But other playwrights, when Hyperbolos[53] let them get a hold of him,
trampled on this wretched one and his mother as well.
Eupolis[54] first brought his Maricas on stage,
distorting my Knights badly, as evil as he is,
adding to it the drunken old woman for the sake of her cordax,   555
the character whom Phrynichos[55] brought up a long time ago,
       and whom the sea monster devoured.
Then Hermippos[56] again wrote about Hyperbolos,
and all others started piling into Hyperbolos,
imitating my similes about the eels.
He who laughs at them, let him not enjoy my work.   560
But if you are pleased with me and my inventions,
you will be considered very wise by future generations.

CHORUS

The highest ruler among the gods,
Almighty Zeus first I call
to my dance;   565
and the great and mighty dispenser of the trident,[57]
the savage one who heaves up
    the earth and the salty sea;
and our great father,
    Aether, the most revered, the nourisher of all lives;   570
and the Charioteer,[58] who occupies
    with his brilliant rays
the open of the earth, a great power
among the mortals and the gods.

CHORUS LEADER

Oh very intelligent spectators, here let your minds concentrate;   575
for we are wronged and have a complaint about you.
We most among all gods benefit your city
and to us alone of the gods you do not sacrifice, or pour libations
to us who watch over you. For if there is any military
expedition which is mindless, then we either thunder or rain.   580
And then, when you were electing as general the god-hated
tanner Paphlagon,[59] we moved our brows and did disastrous
things, the burst of thunder came after lightning,
and the moon left its path, and the sun straight
away drew its wick into its orb   585
and said that it wouldn't shine for you if Kleon was general.
But you elected him. They say that although bad-council
exists in this city, the gods will turn those things,
those that you did wrong, for the best.
And we can teach you too how easily to overcome even
    latest mistakes.   590
If you convict the hungry seagull Kleon of bribery and theft
and then silence him by fastening his neck to the pillory,
and then return to traditional life, even if you made mistakes in some things,
the case will turn out for the best for the city.

CHORUS

Phoebos, Delian king, come   595
near me, and you who dwell on
the high rock of Kythnos;

you, blessed one, who has a golden house in Ephesos,
in which the maidens of the Lydians
    revere you respectfully,   600
and you who are our native goddess,
    the charioteer of the aegis, the patron goddess Athena,
and you who dwell on the rocks of Parnassos
    and enlighten with pine torches,
prominent among the Bacchanals from Delphi,   605
the reveler Dionysos.

CHORUS LEADER

When we were getting ready to rush out of here,
the Moon met us and told us to deliver a message
to the Athenians and their allies;
she said that she was angry because she had suffered misfortunes   610
doing favors for you all, not only with words but with deeds.
First of all, the savings of the month in torches is no less than a drachma,
so that all of you going out in the evening say:
"Don't buy a torch, boy, since the light of the Moon is adequate."
And she says that she does well in other things, but you   615
do not keep the calendar[60] well, but make a mess of confusion,
so that she says that the gods threaten her any time,
when they are cheated of a dinner and go home not
having had their festival on the traditional days.
And then, when you should be sacrificing, you apply torture
    and hold trials.   620
And often when we are starting with a fasting period among the gods,
and when we mourn either for Memnon or Sarpedon,[61]
you pour libations and laugh. This is the reason that although Hyperbolos
was chosen to be the sacred commemorator this
year, he was deprived of his garland by the gods. For this
    way he will know   625
that it is necessary to lead the days of your life according to the Moon.

SOCRATES [*Comes out of the Thinking Establishment*]

By Respiration, by Void, by Air,
I never saw such a peasant,
so tactless, stupid, and forgetful,
who, studying very small petty quibbles,   630
has forgotten them before he has even learned them. But
I'll call him from the door here toward the light.

[*Socrates calls Strepsiades*]

Where are you Strepsiades? Will you come out bringing your bed too?

STREPSIADES [*Comes out with his bed*]

But the bugs won't let me bring it out.

SOCRATES

Hurry up, put it down and concentrate your mind.

STREPSIADES

                                                Look!   635

SOCRATES

Come on, what do you want to learn now
of all the things that you were never taught? Tell me
which—about measures, or words, or rhythms?[62]

STREPSIADES

I'll take measures. For lately I was cheated
by a corn-dealer by three pints.   640

SOCRATES

I am not asking you about that, but what aesthetic measure
is best—the three-measure or the four-measure?[63]

STREPSIADES

None comes before the gallon measure for me.

SOCRATES

You speak nonsense, man.

STREPSIADES

                              Will you bet me
that a gallon does not consist of four quart measures?   645

SOCRATES

To hell with you! What an unteachable peasant you are.
You'd be able to learn about rhythms faster perhaps.

STREPSIADES

How can the rhythms help with my daily food?

SOCRATES

First, it will make you elegant in company,
and make you aware as to which one of the rhythms   650
is the enoplian, and which one again is the digital.

STREPSIADES

Digital?[64] But, by Zeus, I know it.

SOCRATES

                                                  Tell me, then.

STREPSIADES [*He sticks out his middle finger*]

When I was a child, it was this one!

SOCRATES

You are a peasant and a mischievous man.

STREPSIADES

                                          Miserable man,   655
I do not wish to learn any of these things.

SOCRATES

                                        Then what do you want?

STREPSIADES

The other thing, the deceptive argument.

SOCRATES

But it's necessary to learn other things before that,
like which of the quadrupeds are correctly masculine.[65]

STREPSIADES

But I know the masculines, if I am not losing my mind.   660
Ram, he-goat, bull, dog, fowl.

SOCRATES

Do you see what you are doing? You call the female
as well as the male a "fowl."

STREPSIADES

How? Come on.

SOCRATES

How? A "fowl" and a "fowl."

STREPSIADES

By Poseidon, what should I call it?   665

SOCRATES

The one a "hen" and the other a "cock."

STREPSIADES

A hen? Well, by the Air
for this piece of teaching alone
I will fill the surface of your *cardopus* [66] with a full meal of barley.

SOCRATES

Look, once again you confuse the endings. You say   670
cardopus as though it's masculine, but it's feminine.

STREPSIADES

                                        How
am I saying *cardopus* in a masculine way?

SOCRATES

                                   Indeed,
just like the name "Kleonymos."

STREPSIADES

                    What should I do instead? Tell me.

SOCRATES

You think you can treat *cardopus* and Kleonymos in the same way.

STREPSIADES

But, my good man, the *cardopus* did not belong to   675
Kleonymos—he did the kneading in a round mortar.
What should I call it in the future?

SOCRATES

                              What?
Cardope, just like the name "Sostrate."

STREPSIADES

A feminine *cardope*?

SOCRATES

                    That is the right way to say it.

STREPSIADES

So we'd say the *cardope* of Kleonyme.   680

SOCRATES

But still it's necessary to learn about the names,
and which are masculine and which feminine.

STREPSIADES

But I know which ones are feminine

SOCRATES

Tell me, then.

STREPSIADES

Lysilla, Philina, Kleitagora, Demetria.

SOCRATES

And which of the names are masculine?

STREPSIADES

Thousands.   685
Philoxenos, Melesias, Ameinias.

SOCRATES

But these are not masculine, stupid man.

STREPSIADES

They are not masculine for you?

SOCRATES

Not at all.
How would you call to him, if you happen to see Ameinias?

STREPSIADES

How? Just like this: "hey, hey Ameinia."   690

SOCRATES

Don't you see? You call to Ameinias as you'd call to a woman.

STREPSIADES

Isn't that right, since he is afraid to do his military service?
But why should I learn the things that we all know?

SOCRATES

Don't do anything, in the name of Zeus, but lie down here—
[*Socrates shows the bed to Strepsiades*]

STREPSIADES

What shall I do?

SOCRATES

Think about some of your own problems.   695

STREPSIADES

No, I beg you, not there! [*He points out the bed*] If it's necessary
to think about these same things, let me do it on the ground.

SOCRATES

Nowhere but there!

STREPSIADES

Wretched me.
What justice will I give to the bugs today.
[*Socrates goes inside*]

CHORUS

Think and examine every way   700
    spin yourself around and
concentrate your thoughts; and soon, when you fall
    into a difficulty, jump into another

mental idea. And let delightful sleep
    be far from your eyes.   705

STREPSIADES

    Aah, aah!

CHORUS

    What do you suffer? Why are you distressed?

STREPSIADES

    I am perishing, wretched me. From the couch
    the Corinthian bugs[67] are coming out and biting me up,   710
    and are devouring my ribs
    and drinking up my soul
    and pulling my balls up
    and they dig through my ass
    and they waste me away.   715

CHORUS

    Don't grieve too heavily.

STREPSIADES

    But how? when my money
    is gone, my color is gone,
    my soul is gone, my slaves are gone,
    and despite these evils,
    I am singing in the prison   720
    but in a little while I will be gone too.

SOCRATES [*Comes out*]

    What are you doing? Why don't you think?

STREPSIADES

                               Me?

    By Poseidon, I am thinking.

SOCRATES

And what have you thought then?

STREPSIADES

Whether something will be left of me by the moths.   725

SOCRATES

Go to hell!

STREPSIADES

But my good man I have been completely devoured.

CHORUS

You shouldn't be soft, but should cover yourself.
For your mind should discover a means of cheating
and a fraud.

STREPSIADES

Oh me, won't someone throw me
a fraudulent device instead of lambskins?   730

SOCRATES

Come on, now, let me first observe what this guy is doing.
Eh, you, are you sleeping?

STREPSIADES

Not me, by Apollo.

SOCRATES

Do you have any ideas?

STREPSIADES

By Zeus, I do not.

SOCRATES

Nothing at all?

STREPSIADES

Nothing except my cock in my right hand.[68]

SOCRATES

Cover up and think about something fast!   735

STREPSIADES

About what? Tell me this much, Socrates.

SOCRATES

Say the first thing that you yourself wish to discover.

STREPSIADES

You have heard a million times what I want:
not to have to pay any more interest on my debts.

SOCRATES

Go now, cover yourself, and having let your fine   740
mind go, contemplate the subject piece by piece,
investigating and analyzing correctly.

STREPSIADES

Oh, wretched me.

SOCRATES

Don't tremble, and if you hesitate with one of your thoughts
move away and let it go, and another time move it again
back to your mind and weigh it out.   745

STREPSIADES

Oh dearest, sweet Socrates!

SOCRATES

What is it, old man?

STREPSIADES

I have a fraudulent device for avoiding interest.

SOCRATES

Tell me about it.

STREPSIADES

Tell me now—

SOCRATES

About what?

STREPSIADES

What if I bought a sorceress from Thessaly[69]
and had her take down the moon during the night,   750
and then put it in a round case,
just like a mirror, and watched over it.

SOCRATES

How would this benefit you?

STREPSIADES

So that
no longer would the moon rise anywhere,
so I wouldn't have to pay my interest back.

SOCRATES

Why not?   755

STREPSIADES

Money is lent by the month.

SOCRATES

Very well. But I will give you another situation.
If someone pursued a five-talent lawsuit against you,
tell me how would you dispose it?

STREPSIADES

How? How? I don't know. I' ve got to figure this out.   760

SOCRATES

Now don't keep your thought to yourself always,
but let it go aloft,
like a cockchafer tied by the foot.[70]

STREPSIADES

I have discovered the wisest way of taking care of a lawsuit.
You yourself will agree with me.

SOCRATES

                                        What is it?   765

STREPSIADES

Have you already seen at the pharmacist's this stone,[71]
the good one, the transparent one,
with which they light up the fire?

SOCRATES

                          Are you talking about glass?

STREPSIADES

I am. Come on. If I took it
when the clerk was writing the lawsuit in his books,   770
farther off toward the sun I would put it, like this,
and I would melt the writing of my lawsuit.

SOCRATES

Exactly so, by the Graces.

STREPSIADES

                              Oh me, how happy I am that
I have unwritten the five-talent lawsuit against me.

SOCRATES

Come on now, and grasp this next problem fast.

STREPSIADES

                                        Which one?   775

SOCRATES

How would you turn a lawsuit around
when you were about to lose and had no favorable witnesses?

STREPSIADES

Very simply and very easily.

SOCRATES

                    Tell me.

STREPSIADES

                              I am telling you.
If there was a lawsuit before the judge ahead of mine,
I would run away and hang myself.   780

SOCRATES

You are talking nonsense.

STREPSIADES

                              For heaven's sake, no one
will bring a lawsuit against me if I am dead.

SOCRATES

You talk nonsense. Get lost. I will not teach you any more.

STREPSIADES

Why not? Please, Socrates, in the name of the gods.

SOCRATES

But you forget those things that you learn right away.   785
Tell me, what thing were you taught first here?

STREPSIADES

Come on. Let me see. What was the first one?
What was that thing that we knead our daily bread in?
Oh, me, what was it?

SOCRATES

                    Won't you go to hell and get lost,
very forgetful and very stupid old man?   790

STREPSIADES

Oh, what shall I suffer, the wretched one?
I will perish for not learning how to twist my tongue.
Oh Clouds, advise me something good.

CHORUS

We, old man, advise you:
if you have a growing son,   795
send him instead of you to learn.

STREPSIADES

I have a good and fine son;
but he does not want to learn. What shall I do?

CHORUS

And do you give him his own way?

STREPSIADES

> He is grown up and strong, and he is
> from a high-flying race of women, the household of Koesyra.   800
> But I am going for him and if he doesn't want to come
> I will kick him out of the house.
> [*He turns to Socrates*]
> Go in and wait for me for a moment.

CHORUS [*To Strepsiades*]

> Do you feel that soon you will have
>   many blessings from us alone   805
> of the gods? How ready is this man
>   to do everything that you ask him!
> [*Addresses Socrates*]
> And you, knowing that the man is struck
>   and clearly overtaken,
> talk as much as you can, and as   810
>   fast; for it is sometimes the case that somehow these
>   things turn other than you'd expect.

[*Strepsiades has an encounter with Pheidippides*]

STREPSIADES

> No, by Mist, you shall not stay here any longer,
> but go and eat the columns in the house of Megacles.   815

PHEIDIPPIDES

> Oh dear father, what is the matter with you?
> You do not think straight, by Zeus the Olympian god.

STREPSIADES

> Look, look! "The Olympian Zeus!" What stupidity!
> In such an age he believes that Zeus exists.

PHEIDIPPIDES

> Why do you laugh like this?

STREPSIADES

Thinking   820
that you are a child and that you think in an antiquated way.
But come here in order to learn more things, and I'll tell you
something that will make you a man when you learn it,
But do not divulge it to anyone.

PHEIDIPPIDES

What is it?

STREPSIADES

Just now you swore to Zeus.   825

PHEIDIPPIDES

Yes, I did.

STREPSIADES

Do you see how good it is to learn?
Oh Pheidippides, there is no Zeus.

PHEIDIPPIDES

But who is in charge?

STREPSIADES

Vortex rules, having expelled Zeus.

PHEIDIPPIDES

Aah! What are you talking about?

STREPSIADES

Know this the way it is.

PHEIDIPPIDES

Who tells you these things?

STREPSIADES

Socrates, the Melian,[72]   830
and Chaerephon, he who knows the footprints of the fleas.

PHEIDIPPIDES

Are you mad to make such a mistake?
Do you believe the men who look affected with bile-sickness?

STREPSIADES

Talk respectfully,
don't talk evil about men who are capable
and have a brain. Of them not one, because of poverty,   835
ever cut his hair, or anointed himself, or
came to a bathing-room to wash. But you
are wasting my livelihood just as if I were dead.
Come as fast as possible and learn instead of me.

PHEIDIPPIDES

What useful thing could anyone learn from those people?   840

STREPSIADES

Truly? As many wisdoms as there are among men.
You'll learn yourself how stupid and thick you are.
But wait for me for a little bit here.

PHEIDIPPIDES

Oh! what shall I do now that my father has gone crazy?
Which of the two: should I take him to the court for his madness,   845
or should I tell the coffin-makers of his affliction?

STREPSIADES [*Returns holding a hen and a rooster*]

Come, let me see, what do you think that this is? Tell me.

PHEIDIPPIDES

A fowl.

STREPSIADES

Good. And this one here?

PHEIDIPPIDES

A fowl.

STREPSIADES

Both the same? You are to be laughed at.
Do not say this in the future, but call this one   850
a "hen," and that one a "cock."

PHEIDIPPIDES

A hen? Did you learn these smart things
when you entered the place of the children of the earth?[73]

STREPSIADES

And much more. But every time, whatever I learned,
I would forget right away because of my old age.   855

PHEIDIPPIDES

Because of these things you even lost your cloak?

STREPSIADES

But I have not lost it. I have invested it in knowledge.

PHEIDIPPIDES

And where have you fed your shoes, oh stupid you?

STREPSIADES

Just like Pericles,[74] I have lost them for essential purposes.
But come, walk, let us go. And after listening to your   860
father, you can go wrong if you want. I know that when you
were six years old, I listened to you when you lisped.
When I received my first obol from jury duty,[75]
I bought you a toy cart for the Diasia.

PHEIDIPPIDES [*He follows Strepsiades to the Thinkery*]

Eventually you'll be sorry for this.   865

STREPSIADES

It's good that you listened.
                          Here, here, Socrates,
come out. I bring you the son of mine here
who has listened to me but is unwilling.

SOCRATES [*Comes out*]

                                    He is still an infant
and not skilled in the ropes and lashings here.

PHEIDIPPIDES

May you be hanged and receive a lashing yourself.   870

STREPSIADES

Won't you go to hell? Do you curse your teacher?

SOCRATES

Look! I am hanging. How silly he sounded
with his lips opened up.
How will he ever learn to evade a lawsuit
or summons, or bombastic persuasion?   875
Although even Hyperbolos learned these—for a talent.

STREPSIADES

Teach him without worrying. He is naturally clever.
Even when he was a small boy, this big,
he made clay houses and curved boats in the house   880
and made carts of fig wood and frogs of pomegranate peel,
      can you imagine how?
Just as he will learn those arguments,[76]
the just one, whatever it is, and the unjust,
which can overthrow the just argument by pleading an unjust cause.
And if not both, at least he'll learn to use the unjust argument
      very skillfully.   885

SOCRATES

He will learn from the two arguments in person;
I shall go away.

STREPSIADES

Remember this now, that
he ought to be able to argue against every kind of justice.

[*Socrates and Strepsiades exit and the two Arguments enter*]

JUST ARGUMENT [*To Unjust Argument*]

Walk this way. Show yourself
to the audience, although you are rude.   890

UNJUST ARGUMENT

Go as you like. For I would rather
destroy you very much in public.

JUST ARGUMENT

You will destroy me? Who are you?

UNJUST ARGUMENT

An argument.

JUST ARGUMENT

But a lesser one.

UNJUST ARGUMENT

But I will conquer you,
who says that you are better than me.

JUST ARGUMENT

Doing what wise thing?   895

UNJUST ARGUMENT

Devising new ideas.

JUST ARGUMENT [*He points to the audience*]

But new ideas are blooming
among these fools.

UNJUST ARGUMENT

No, they are wise.

JUST ARGUMENT

I will utterly destroy you.

UNJUST ARGUMENT

Tell me, what are you going to do?

JUST ARGUMENT

I will talk about just things.   900

UNJUST ARGUMENT

But I will turn them around by saying the opposite.
For I say that Justice doesn't exists.

JUST ARGUMENT

Are you saying that it does not exist?

UNJUST ARGUMENT

Come on, where is it then?

JUST ARGUMENT

With the gods.[77]

UNJUST ARGUMENT

Then, since Justice exists, how come Zeus
did not perish for imprisoning
his father?[78]   905

JUST ARGUMENT

Oh, this is getting worse.
It's making me sick. Give me a basin.

UNJUST ARGUMENT

You are senile and maladjusted.

JUST ARGUMENT

And you are a shameless fag.

UNJUST ARGUMENT

You are giving me bouquets!

JUST ARGUMENT

And a beggar.   910

UNJUST ARGUMENT

You garland me with lilies!

JUST ARGUMENT

And a father beater.

UNJUST ARGUMENT

You do not know it, but you sprinkle me with gold.

JUST ARGUMENT

In the old days these insults were not gold but resembled lead.

UNJUST ARGUMENT

But now they're an embellishment to me.

JUST ARGUMENT

You are gross.

UNJUST ARGUMENT

And you are antiquated.   915

JUST ARGUMENT

Because of you, none of the
youngsters wishes to go to school.
In time, it will be known to the Athenians
that you teach these things which have made them fools.

UNJUST ARGUMENT

You are grubby.

JUST ARGUMENTS

And you're fancy,   920
although you used to be poor before,
saying that you are a Mysian Telephos,[79]
eating knavish opinions
from a little bag.

UNJUST ARGUMENT

Oh, what "wisdom"—

JUST ARGUMENT

Oh, what "lunacy"—   925

UNJUST ARGUMENT

In what you have said!

JUST ARGUMENT

                         In your city,
    which feeds you
    while you corrupt its youths.

UNJUST ARGUMENTS

    You, being like Kronos, will not educate him.
    [*He points to Pheidippides*].

JUST ARGUMENT

    I will, if it's necessary to be saved   930
    and not to exercise speech only.

UNJUST ARGUMENT   [*To Pheidippides*]

    Come here, and let him go crazy.

JUST ARGUMENT

    You'll weep if you lay a hand on him.

CHORUS

    Enough of fighting and abuse.
    [*To Just Argument*]
        You show those things that you   935
        taught to people in the past,
    [*To Unjust Argument*]
        and you, the new education,
        so that if he hears both opposing
        arguments he may choose which school he will attend.

JUST ARGUMENT

    I want to do these things.

UNJUST ARGUMENT

                         And I want to, also.

CHORUS

Come now, who will speak first?   940

UNJUST ARGUMENT

I shall give the floor to him;
and then, on the basis of what he says,
I shall shoot him with new phrases and ideas,
and at the end, if he keeps muttering,   945
just as if he has been stung by hornets all over
his entire face and eyes,
he will perish by my arguments.

CHORUS [*To the audience*]

Now these two will show themselves, they who rely
      on very capable   950
arguments and thoughts
      and opinionated cogitations.
And he who talks the best of
      these two will prove himself.
For now everything here   955
      is at stake for learning
in regard to which, for my friends,
      this is the greatest contest.

[*To Just Argument*]
But oh, you who garlanded the men of the past with
      many good customs,
seek with your voice, in the tone that you rejoice
      to explain your own nature to us.   960

JUST ARGUMENT

I will tell how the old education was fixed
when I spoke and justice flourished and moderation was apportioned.
First, it was a rule that no one should hear the voice of a screaming boy.
The students had to walk through the streets in a good order to the
      music of the cithara player,
and naked, even if it snowed heavily.   965
Then, once again, the master would have them learn the song
in advance, not keeping their thighs together,[80]
either "Pallas the terrible sacker of cities" or "A far-reaching
      cry,"

stretching the harmony that their fathers gave them.
And if one of them indulged in buffoonery or he bent   970
with a turning like the moderns do, those hard-bending twists
    in the style of Phrynis,[81]
he was thrashed hard, ruined for obliterating the Muses.
And when they were sitting down at the gymnast's place it was
a rule that the boys would cover their thighs, so that they
wouldn't expose to outsiders anything that was hard.[82]
And then, once again, when they stood up, they swept away   975
and took care not to leave the imprint of their manhood behind
    for their lovers.
And no boy would anoint himself below the navel,
    so that
dew and pubic hair would bloom among his genitals just like in the cheeks.
Nor did he make his voice soft toward his lover
or walk making eyes and promoting himself.[83]   980
Nor was he allowed to pick the head of the radish when he was dining,
nor to snatch the dill of his elders, or their celery,
nor to eat dainties, nor to laugh, nor to have his legs one over the other.

UNJUST ARGUMENT

How antiquated, from the time of Dipoleia,[84] filled with cicadas,
Cedeides[85] and Bouphonia.[86]

JUST ARGUMENT

                    But these are the principles   985
from which my education bred the men who fought at Marathon.[87]
And you teach the modern ones from the beginning how to wrap
    themselves with their cloaks,
so that I want to hang myself when it is necessary that they
    dance during the Panathenaea[88]
holding their shield in front of their hams without caring about Tritogeneia.[89]
Because of these things, my young man, choose me, the Just
    Argument, with courage,   990
and you will no doubt hate the agora and abstain from the bathing places,
and be ashamed of shameful things and burn up when someone
    makes fun of you,
and get up from your seat for the elders, when they approach,
and not contrive against your parents, and not do any
other shameful thing that would defile the statue
    of Shame.[90]   995
Nor dart to the place of the dancing girls, so that when you are gaping,

being struck by an apple, thrown to you by a little whore, you are
    deprived of your reputation,
or contradict your father in anything, nor call him Iapetos[91]
and be contemptuous of his years, those years devoted to raising you
    since you were an infant.

UNJUST ARGUMENT

If he persuades you with this, my young man, then, by Dionysos   1000
you will resemble the sons of Hippocrates[92] and they will call
    you a booby.

JUST ARGUMENT

But gleaming and blooming you will be waiting for your time
    in the gymnasium,
not chattering in the agora in coarse, thorny jests, like the
    modern ones,
nor dragged in for a greedy-pettifogging-barefooted knavish dispute,
but going to the Academy under the sacred olives you will race   1005
with an intelligent companion garlanded with a white reed,
smelling of begony and idleness and shedding poplar leaves,
delightful in the spring time when the plane tree whispers to the elm.
If you do these things which I tell you
and turn your mind to them   1010
you will always have
a gleaming breast, gleaming skin,
broad shoulders, a little tongue
a big ass and a small cock.
But if you pursue those principles of the modern ones,   1015
first you will have
pale skin, small shoulders,
small chest, a big tongue,
a small ass and a long decree.
They will persuade you to consider everything   1020
dishonest as decent, and the decent as dishonest,
and in addition to these things they will
infect you with the brutal lust of Antimachos.[93]

CHORUS

Oh you who labor with
    famous, high-towering wisdom,   1025

how sweet among your words
    is the bloom of virtue.
Happy, indeed, were the people who lived then.
[*To the Unjust Argument*]
    And because of this, you who have a refined art,   1030
    it's necessary to tell you something new:
        the man has got a good reputation.

    It seems that you need powerful arguments against him
    if you are to overcome the man and not be liable to ridicule.   1035

UNJUST ARGUMENT

    Indeed, I was choking before inside and decided
    to destroy all these things with a counter-argument.
    I was named Unjust Argument for this very reason
    amongst the thinkers: I first contrived
    to talk against the established customs and the lawsuits.   1040
[*To Pheidippides*]
    And this is worth more than ten thousand staters—
    to choose the weaker case and then to win.
    And look how I'll talk about education, which he trusts,
    he who first said that he wouldn't allow you to bathe in hot water.
[*To Just Argument*]
    And what reason do you have to object to hot baths?   1045

JUST ARGUMENT

    Because they're very unmanly and make a man a coward.

UNJUST ARGUMENT

    Hold on. Right away I have you in a waistlock which you can't escape.
    Tell me, among Zeus' children whom do you consider the
    best-hearted and to have suffered most labors?

JUST ARGUMENT

    I do not judge any man better than Heracles.   1050

UNJUST ARGUMENT

    Where then have you seen cold Heraclean baths?[94]
    But who was more manly than he?

JUST ARGUMENT

These are the things that
the young men are always talking about all day long, which
make the bathing place full and the wrestling place empty.

UNJUST ARGUMENT

Then you blame their waste of time in the agora, but I
    congratulate it.   1055
For if it were wicked, Homer would never make
Nestor,[95] nor all wise men, marketplace haunters.
Then let me go from here to the tongue, which this one here
says it is not useful for the young to train. I say it is useful.
And again he says that it's necessary to be modest, a second
    great evil.   1060
Since when have you seen anything good done for the
modest ones? Say it and contradict me by naming it.

JUST ARGUMENT

Many people. Peleus[96] got his knife because of modesty.

UNJUST ARGUMENT

A knife? The wretched man, he received a ridiculous profit.
And Hyperbolos now, from the lamps he sold, he received tons
    of talents   1065
because of his shrewdness but, by Zeus, not a knife.

JUST ARGUMENT

And because of his virtue Peleus married Thetis.[97]

UNJUST ARGUMENT

And then she left him and went away[98] for he wasn't vigorous,
not a sweet lover to last all night long under the covers.
A woman likes to be treated wantonly. And you are from the line
    of Kronos.   1070
For just think, oh young man, of everything that virtue entails
and of how many pleasures you are about to be deprived;

boys, women, kottabos,[99] good food, drinking, laughter.
What is it worth for you to live if you are deprived of these things?
Well, from here I will proceed to the needs of nature.   1075
Let's say you make a mistake, you fall in love, you commit adultery,
    and then you are caught.
You are ruined; for you'll be too weak to argue. But consorting
with me you may indulge your nature, leap and laugh and consider
    nothing shameful.
For if you are caught as an adulterer, you'll tell the husband
that you have committed nothing wrong, and then transfer blame
    to Zeus.   1080
He is a slave of love and women,
and since you are mortal, how would it be possible to be stronger
    than a god?

JUST ARGUMENT

And what if listening to you he gets the radish treatment[100] and he
    is plucked with ashes?
Will he have any argument to support himself and not be wide-assed?

UNJUST ARGUMENT

And if he is wide-assed, what evil will he suffer?   1085

JUST ARGUMENT

Can he suffer that's worse than this?

UNJUST ARGUMENT

What would you say then if you are refuted by me in this?

JUST ARGUMENT

I'll shut up. What else?

UNJUST ARGUMENT
                    Come on now, tell me
from which kind of people do the advocates come?

JUST ARGUMENT

From the wide-assed.

UNJUST ARGUMENT

                              I agree.   1090
    And then from what type do tragedy playwrights come?

JUST ARGUMENT

    From the wide-assed.

UNJUST ARGUMENT

                        You speak very well.
    And from which kind of people do the demagogues come?

JUST ARGUMENT

    From the wide-assed.

UNJUST ARGUMENT

                                   Then,
    do you see that you've said nothing?   1095
    And look who are the majority among the spectators.

JUST ARGUMENT

    I see, indeed.

UNJUST ARGUMENT

                        Then, what do you see?

JUST ARGUMENT

    In the name of the gods, the majority
    are the wide-assed; I know
        that this one is, and those people there,
    and that one with the long hair.   1100

UNJUST ARGUMENT

    What do you say then?

JUST ARGUMENT

I am defeated. Oh buggers,
for heaven's sake receive my cloak,
    I am deserting to you.

UNJUST ARGUMENT [*To Strepsiades*]

Well? Which of us do you want to take   1105
your son away? Should I teach him the art of speaking?

STREPSIADES

Teach him and chastise him and remember how
to furnish him with a good edge for me, with one
side for lawsuits, and the other side of his jaws
furnished with an edge for greater affairs.   1110

UNJUST ARGUMENT

Do not worry, you'll carry him back a skilled sophist.

PHEIDIPPIDES

I think a paleface and a wretched man.

CHORUS [*To Strepsiades*]

Go now. And I think that you
    will regret these things.

CHORUS LEADER [*To the audience*]

We wish to tell you how the judges will benefit, if they   1115
help this chorus in the way it deserves.
For, first of all, if you wish to rejuvenate your fields in season,
we will rain for you first, and later for the other people.
Then we will protect your crops and your producing vines,
so that they will not be damaged either by drought or excessive
    rain.   1120
But if someone who is mortal dishonors us who are goddesses,
let him beware of the evils that he will suffer from us
when he gets neither wine nor anything else from his land.

For when the olives and the vines sprout, they
will be cut off. We'll shoot them with sling-shots.[101]   1125
And if we see him making bricks, we will rain, and the tiling
of his roof we shall destroy with round hailstones.
And if he ever gets married himself or one of his relatives or friends does,[102]
we shall rain the entire night, so that perhaps he will wish
to find himself in Egypt rather than to have given a wrong verdict.   1130

STREPSIADES [*He counts on his fingers*]

Five days, four days, three days; and after this the second day;[103]
the one that I have feared most of all days,
which makes me dread and turns my stomach.
Immediately after this one comes the old-and-new day.[104]
For everyone whom I happen to owe swears that he   1135
will take a deposit[105] against me and says that he will crush me
     and destroy me.
And when I ask modestly and justly, "Oh dear, won't you take
this payment now, and postpone the other one, and wipe out
     the other one?"
they say that they will never accept such a deal, and abuse me,   1140
as though I am dishonest, and say that they will bring me to court.
Let them sue now! For I care very little,
if Pheidippides has learned how to speak well.
Soon I will know. Let me knock at the Thinking Establishment.
Boy, hey, boy, boy!

SOCRATES

                         I greet you Strepsiades.   1145

STREPSIADES

The same to you. But take this first of all.[106]
[*Strepsiades gives Socrates a gift*]
For it is necessary in some way to express respect for the teacher.
And tell me if my son has learned that argument,
the one you brought out just now.

SOCRATES

He has learned it.

STREPSIADES

                    Very well, oh Almighty Fraud!   1150

SOCRATES

So that you can avoid any lawsuit that you wish.

STREPSIADES

Even if witnesses were present when I borrowed the money?

SOCRATES

The more the better, even if there are one thousand of them.

STREPSIADES

Then I will scream an overpowering
scream. Oh lament, you money lenders, for   1155
you yourselves and the principal and the interests of interests.
For you may not act against me with evil,
such is the son who is nourished
in these quarters
shining with a two-edged tongue,   1160
my defense, the savior in my house, a harm to my enemies,
the dispeller of his father's great evils;
you should run and call him from within.
[*Socrates goes inside*]
My child, boy, come out from the house,   1165
listen to your father.

SOCRATES [*Brings Pheidippides out*]

This is the man.

STREPSIADES

Oh dear one, oh dear one!

SOCRATES

Take him and leave.

STREPSIADES

Oh my son, oh my son!   1170

Oh, oh!
How pleased I am first to see your pallor.
Now, a first glance shows that you are negative
and contradictory, and this fashionable look
absolutely blossoms—you seem to say "what are you talking about?"
and you look wronged when you are doing the wrong,
even committing a crime, I'm sure.   1175
There is a genuine Attic grace in your face.
Now you save me—since you've ruined me.

PHEIDIPPIDES

And what are you afraid of?

STREPSIADES

                                    The old-and-the-new day.

PHEIDIPPIDES [*Arrogantly*]

But does an old-and-new day really exist?

STREPSIADES

It's the one on which they say they will put their deposits against
    me.   1180

PHEIDIPPIDES

Let those who put them, lose them, then. For there is no way
that one day can become two days.

STREPSIADES

It isn't possible?

PHEIDIPPIDES

                    How can it be unless a woman can
become old and young at the same time?

STREPSIADES

But it's customary.

PHEIDIPPIDES

I think that they don't know what   1185
the law clearly means.

STREPSIADES

And what does it mean?

PHEIDIPPIDES

Old Solon[107] was a friend of the people—that is, the debtors—by nature.

STREPSIADES

So for him somehow there wasn't any old-and-new day?

PHEIDIPPIDES

He fixed the summons paid in two different days,
the old-and-the-new day,   1190
so that the deposits would be made during the New Moon.

STREPSIADES

Why did he add the old day?

PHEIDIPPIDES

So that, my good man,
the defendants who were present for that day
would settle voluntarily in advance; otherwise they would
be a bit disturbed early in the morning of the New Moon.   1195

STREPSIADES

How come then the magistrates do not accept deposits
on the New Moon, but only on the old-and-the-new day?

PHEIDIPPIDES

It seems to me that they are as ready as the Tasters;[108]
they want to take away the deposits as fast
as possible, and for this reason they claim them a day in advance.   1200

STREPSIADES [*To the audience*]

Very well. Oh wretched fools, why are you sitting, stupid ones,
are you stones, profits for us, the intellectuals,
quantity, otherwise sheep, a heap of jars?
So that I should sing a song for myself and this son
of mine and our happiness.   1205
"Oh Strepsiades, what a blessed man
you were born, what a wise man
and what son you are raising,"
so will say my friends and demesmen
being envious if you win   1210
        my lawsuit with your speeches.
But first I wish to take you inside to feast.

[*The First Creditor with his witness enter*]

PASIAS

Then how is it necessary that a man let drop his money?
Never—but it would have been better to put blushes away   1215
immediately then rather than get into trouble,
when because of my money I dragged you here
to witness a summons, and in addition, I'll become
the enemy of this fellow demesman.
But I will never disgrace my country as long as I live—   1220
I summon Strepsiades.

STREPSIADES

                            Who is there?

PASIAS

I have come for the old-and-the-new day.

STREPSIADES [*To the audience*]

I call you to witness
that he summoned me for two different days.
[*To the creditor*]   For what?

PASIAS

For the twelve minas that you borrowed,
when you bought the gray horse.

STREPSIADES

A horse? Did you hear him?   1225
Me, who you all know hate horse racing.

PASIAS

And by Zeus, you swore to the gods that you would give me my money.

STREPSIADES

By Zeus, because Pheidippides did not yet know
the argument that cannot be overthrown.

PASIAS

And now because of this, are you thinking of denying the debt?   1230

STREPSIADES

But what other benefit would I get from his training?

PASIAS

And now in the name of the gods you want to deny this oath,
in whatever place I may bid you?

STREPSIADES

What gods?

PASIAS

Zeus, Hermes, and Poseidon.

STREPSIADES

By Zeus, and I
would even add three obols to the debt for the sake of
unswearing it all over again.   1235

PASIAS

May you be ruined because of your rudeness!

STREPSIADES

You could benefit from being rubbed down with salt.

PASIAS

Oh, now you mock me!

STREPSIADES

Your paunch holds six gallons.

PASIAS

By Zeus the great and the gods,
you will not escape from me.

STREPSIADES

I am incredibly amused by "the gods,"   1240
and swearing to Zeus makes you ridiculous to those who know.

PASIAS

Indeed you will have to pay for these things someday.
But now let me go away with an answer:
will you give me the money or not?

STREPSIADES

Keep quiet;
I shall give you a reply immediately.   1245
[*He exits momentarily*]

PASIAS [*To his witness*]

What do you think he will do? Do you think he'll give it to me?

STREPSIADES [*Re-enters with a kneading-tray*]

Where is this man who demands money from me? Tell me,
what is this?

PASIAS

What is this? It's a *cardopus*.

STREPSIADES

And you ask for money, being such a fool?
I wouldn't give an obol to anyone   1250
who calls a *"cardope"* a *"cardopus."*

PASIAS

You won't give it?

STREPSIADES

Not knowingly, no, I won't.
Why don't you hurry up and pack yourself out of the door?

PASIAS

I am going and know this—that
I shall lodge the deposits as sure as I am alive.   1255
[*He exits*]

STREPSIADES [*Screaming after him*]

Then you'll throw the deposit away along with the twelve minas I owe you.
Although I do not want this to happen to you just because
you well-meaningly call a *"cardopus"* a *"cardope."*

[*The Second Creditor enters*]

AMYNIAS

Woe is me! Woe is me!

STREPSIADES

Here.
Who is complaining? Was it   1260
one of Carcinos'[109] deities that spoke?

AMYNIAS

Do you want to know who I am?
I am a wretched man.

STREPSIADES

Then just go away.

AMYNIAS

Oh cruel deity! Oh fortunes shattered to pieces
because of my horses! Oh Pallas, how you ruined me!   1265

STREPSIADES

What harm has Tlempolemos[110] ever done to you?

AMYNIAS

Don't joke with me, but tell your son
to give me back the money that he got from me.
Otherwise I will continue to act this way.

STREPSIADES

What money?

AMYNIAS

The money that he borrowed.   1270

STREPSIADES

It seems to me that you have it badly, indeed.

AMYNIAS

For heaven's sake, I fell out of my chariot while driving.

STREPSIADES

Then why do you speak as though you have fallen off a donkey?[111]

AMYNIAS

Do I speak foolishly if I wish to get my money back?

STREPSIADES

Do you think you'll get your sanity back?

AMYNIAS

What?   1275

STREPSIADES

It seems to me that your brain has had a shaking.

AMYNIAS

By Hermes, you'll get a summons from me
if you don't give me the money.

STREPSIADES

Tell me now,
which of these two things do you believe—that every time
that Zeus rains, the water is always new, or that the sun   1280
draws the same water up again and again from down here?

AMYNIAS

I do not know which of the two is true, nor do I care.

STREPSIADES

And how are you entitled to get your money back,
if you know nothing about natural phenomena?

AMYNIAS

If you're short of money, give me   1285
the interest.

STREPSIADES

What kind of animal is this "interest"?

AMYNIAS

What else than the money always growing
more and more every month and day
while time is flowing?

STREPSIADES

You speak well.
Do you then think that the sea   1290
is bigger now than before?

AMYNIAS

By Zeus, it's equal to what it was.
It's against the laws of nature for it to be more.

STREPSIADES

You miserable man, if it doesn't get bigger
while rivers are flowing in why do you wish
to make your money more?   1295
Won't you get out of my house?
[*He calls inside*]
Bring me the horse goad.

AMYNIAS

I'll remember these things.

STREPSIADES

Go away, What do you care? Won't you get out, oh, *San*-branded horse?

AMYNIAS

This isn't a curse?

STREPSIADES

                                        Won't you get out?
I will lay the goad on you and your *San*-branded ass.   1300
Are you leaving? For I was about to drive you off
like a chariot.
[*Strepsiades exits*]

CHORUS

What a wretched thing is it to fall in love with swindling?
    For this old man is enamored with it
and wishes to deprive them   1305
of the money which he has borrowed.
And it is certain that today
    he'll get something,
    this sophist will have the tables
    turned on him, be hurt
    by his own trickery.   1310

For I think that right away he will find
what he had looked for in the past—
that his son is skilled in arguing
for contradictory opinions
against justice—so that   1315
    he wins over all people,
    even his relatives, even if he speaks
    in favor of wicked things. And perhaps,
    perhaps he may wish
to shut his son up.   1320

[*Strepsiades comes out of the house followed by Pheidippides*]

STREPSIADES

Help, help!
Oh friends and neighbors and fellow demesmen,
come to my help! I am being thoroughly beaten up!
Oh wretched me, my head, my jaws!
Oh miserable son, are you hitting your father?

PHEIDIPPIDES

Yes, father. 1325

STREPSIADES

Do you see that he even admits that he is beating me?

PHEIDIPPIDES

Very much so.

STREPSIADES

You wretched one, father-beater, house-breaker.

PHEIDIPPIDES

Say it again. Say worse things.
Don't you know that I enjoy hearing curses?

STREPSIADES

Oh wide-assed!

PHEIDIPPIDES

Give me more bouquets! 1330

STREPSIADES

Are you beating up your father?

PHEIDIPPIDES

And by Zeus, I'll even prove
that I am beating you justly.

STREPSIADES

Oh wretched one,
how could it be just to beat up your father?

PHEIDIPPIDES

I'll prove to you how I can conquer you in argument.

STREPSIADES

You'll prove me wrong about this?

PHEIDIPPIDES

Very much so, and easily.   1335
Choose which of the two arguments you want.

STREPSIADES

Which of the arguments?

PHEIDIPPIDES

The Just or the Unjust?

STREPSIADES

By Zeus, I am the one who had you taught
how to argue against just causes. Do you think
you're about to persuade me that it's   1340
just and fair that a father is beaten up by his sons?

PHEIDIPPIDES

I'll convince you, so that
you haven't a doubt about it.

STREPSIADES

I'd like to hear what you have to say, indeed.

CHORUS [*To Strepsiades*]

You'd better think, old man, how   1345
you'll defeat this fellow.
For if he did not have anything to rely on, he wouldn't
be so hubristic.
But there is something that makes him bold. For the
insolence of the man is obvious.   1350

But first, it's necessary to tell the chorus where the quarrel
started; and you should do this in detail.

STREPSIADES

I will tell you where we first started to rail at
one another. When we were eating inside, as you know,
I asked him to take the lyre in order to sing a song   1355
of Simonides, "How the ram was shorn."[112] And he immediately
said that to play the guitar and to sing while drinking
is old-fashioned, just like a woman grinding barley.[113]

PHEIDIPPIDES

You should have been beaten and trampled,
bidding me to sing just as if I were a cicada entertaining.   1360

STREPSIADES

He said the same thing then,
and he said that Simonides is a bad poet.
At the beginning, I was tolerant.
And then I asked him to take a myrtle-branch
and recite something from the works of Aeschylos.[114]
      But right away he said: 1365
"I think that Aeschylos is the first among the poets—
more full of noise, incoherence, bombast, creator of big, ragged words."
How did you think my heart palpitated at that?
But I said, biting back my anger: "Then recite something from
these modern poets, whatever their wise things are."   1370

And immediately he sang some poem of Euripides, about
a brother having it with his sister from the same mother,[115] the evil-mouthed!
I couldn't take it any longer, but smote him with
many shameful words. From there on, as is obvious,
we exchanged insults with one another, and then he jumped up   1375
and knocked me, and banged me, and choked me, and pulverized me.

PHEIDIPPIDES

    Wasn't it right, you who don't praise Euripides
as a very wise man?

STREPSIADES [*Sarcastically*]

        Isn't this guy smart? What can I say?
I'll be beaten once again.

PHEIDIPPIDES

            By Zeus, you'd deserve it!

STREPSIADES

    And how would I deserve it? I who raised you, shameless idiot,   1380
who understood all your lisping, whatever you meant.
And if you said "bru,"[116] I knew and gave you drink;
and when you asked for "mama,"[117] I came to you bringing bread;
and no sooner had you said "kaka," but I grabbed you and
brought you outside and held you. And you now are   1385
ready to choke me. You wouldn't
    even take me outside when I
    cried and screamed that I wanted
    to shit, miserable one, but you choked me
    until I crapped on the spot.   1390

CHORUS

    I think that the hearts of the young
will jump with what Pheidippides will answer.
For if he has worked on these things
and he persuades us after talking to us,
then for the skin of the elderly we wouldn't   1395
even give a chick pea![118]

[*To Pheidippides*]
    It is your job to find some means of persuasion, oh you the
    shifter and upheaver of argumentation, so that we may think
        that what you say is right.

PHEIDIPPIDES

    How sweet it is to talk about new and right things
    and to be able to look down on the established laws.   1400
    For when I paid attention to racing alone
    not even three words could I say, before making a blunder;
    but now, since he himself made me stop these things,
    and I am familiar with fine ideas, and arguments and judgments,
    I know to teach how it is just to punish your own father.   1405

STREPSIADES

    Ride your horses then, by Zeus. It's better for me to nourish
    a team of four horses than to be pulverized and beaten up.

PHEIDIPPIDES

    I shall return to the point in the argument where you interrupted me,
    and ask you this first: did you beat me up when I was a boy?

STREPSIADES

    Yes I did, with good intentions and for your own good.

PHEIDIPPIDES

                                    Tell me about it.   1410
    Isn't it just for me to mean well likewise by beating you,
    since this is to mean well—to beat someone up?
    For how is it possible that your body is immune from blows,
    and mine was not? I was born a free man like you.
    "The children cry, do you think the father shouldn't?"[119]   1415
    You will say that it's conventional that this is done to a child.
    And I will reply that the elderly are twice children.
    It seems that the elderly should be punished more than the
    young inasmuch as it's less natural for them to make mistakes.

STREPSIADES

But it's not conventional anywhere that a father suffers this.   1420

PHEIDIPPIDES

Wasn't this law man-made in the first place?
Didn't a man just like you and me persuade the elderly by talking to them?
So why shouldn't I make a new law for the sons
in the future to hit back at their fathers?
We'll forgive them the many blows that we received before   1425
the law was made. We'll grant them a pardon for those.
Think about the roosters and the other animals and
how they defend themselves against their fathers; how do
animals differ from us, except that they do not propose decrees?

STREPSIADES

Why then, since you imitate the roosters in everything,   1430
don't you eat their shit and sleep on a bench?

PHEIDIPPIDES

My good man, it's not the same, nor could it seem so to Socrates.

STREPSIADES

Do not hit me because of these things. Otherwise you will blame
    yourself someday.

PHEIDIPPIDES

And how?

STREPSIADES

                    If I am allowed to chastise you,
you can beat your son, if you have one.

PHEIDIPPIDES

                              But if I don't,   1435
you'll have punished me, and you'll die laughing at me.

STREPSIADES [*Addresses the audience*]

> To me, oh men of today, he seems to speak justly.
> I think that we should yield to the young what is fair;
> Yes, it's fitting that we be punished, if we don't do what is just.

PHEIDIPPIDES

> And consider another opinion.

STREPSIADES

>   I am perishing from this one.   1440

PHEIDIPPIDES

> But perhaps this will ease your burden.

STREPSIADES

> How? Show me in what way you can benefit me in something.

PHEIDIPPIDES

> I will beat up mother just as I did you.

STREPSIADES

>   What are you saying? What are you talking about?
> This is another, greater evil.

PHEIDIPPIDES

>   What if I prove to you,
> using the unjust argument,
> that it's necessary to beat my mother up?[120]   1445

STREPSIADES

> What else? If you do that,
> you can throw yourself
> into the Barathron[121] along with Socrates
> and the Unjust Argument!   1450

[*He addresses the Chorus*]
   I have suffered this because of you, Clouds,
   entrusting all my affairs to you.

CHORUS

   You yourself are responsible for these things,
   you who turned[122] yourself toward evil actions.   1455

STREPSIADES

   Why didn't you tell me about these things then,
   instead of enticing me like a rustic, old man?

CHORUS

   We do these things every time
   we discover that someone is in love with evil things;
   we cast him into misery,   1460
   until he learns how to be afraid of the gods.

STREPSIADES

   Woe is me! Hard words Clouds, but fair;
   for it wasn't right to evade payment of the money
   which I borrowed. [*He addresses Pheidippides*]
                                    So now, dearest one,
   come with me and let Chaerephon, the miserable one,   1465
   and Socrates perish, they who cheated both you and me.

PHEIDIPPIDES

   But I couldn't wrong my teachers.

STREPSIADES

   Yes, yes, have fear of paternal Zeus.

PHEIDIPPIDES

   Look at that! "The paternal Zeus!" How out of date you are!
   For who is Zeus?

STREPSIADES

He exists.

PHEIDIPPIDES

He doesn't exist, no,   1470
not since Vortex who has expelled Zeus rules.

STREPSIADES

He has not expelled him. But I thought he had
because of this vortex-cup.[123] How stupid I was
to suppose that a cup was a god.

PHEIDIPPIDES

Rave and talk to yourself here.   1475
[*He exits*]

STREPSIADES

What insanity! How angry I was
when I discarded the gods because of Socrates.
But, oh beloved Hermes, do not be angry at me,
and do not destroy me, but forgive me
if I have acted insanely with my idle talk.   1480
And become my councilor: should I prosecute them
by writing a lawsuit? what do you think is best?
You advise me right: not to go to law
but as soon as possible to burn the house[124]
of the insolent ones. Here, here, Xanthias,   1485
come out and bring a ladder and an axe,
and then go on top of the Thinking Establishment
and chop the roof, if you love your master,
until you bring the house down on them.
And let someone bring a lit torch to me.   1490
I will make someone pay a penalty today for these
things that they did to me, even if they are very insolent.

FIRST STUDENT

Help! Help!

STREPSIADES

Oh torch, your task is to send a huge flame.

FIRST STUDENT

Hey man, what are you doing?

STREPSIADES

What I am doing? What else than
chopping logic from the posts of the house?   1495

SECOND STUDENT

Help! Who is burning our house?

STREPSIADES

The same man whose cloak you stole.

SECOND STUDENT

You'll destroy us! You'll destroy us!

STREPSIADES

That's exactly what I want,
if the axe doesn't betray my hopes   1500
or I fall beforehand somehow and break my neck.

SOCRATES

Eh, you! What are you doing on the roof?

STREPSIADES

I walk on the air and look down on the sun.

SOCRATES

Oh, wretched stupid me, I am choking!

SECOND STUDENT

And I, wretched man, burn up alive.   1505

STREPSIADES

Why did you insult the gods
and inspect the seat of the moon?
Chase them, hit them, strike them for many causes,
but mostly so that they get to know how they insulted the gods.

CHORUS

Lead the way out; for we have danced enough for today!   1510

Notes

1   During the Peloponnesian War, an ill-treated slave who ran away could be safe if he reached enemy territory.

2   Long hair was fashionable among the rich and characteristic of only those people who could maintain a horse—the equestrian social class.

3   The ancient Greek calendar was based on the lunar year and the Attic months had 29 and 30 days, alternatively. Since interest was reckoned monthly, a moon in its twenties would warn debtors to come up with their payments.

4   A silver mina was approximately 437 grams and was equivalent to 100 drachmas.

5   The letter *koppa* was used as a brand mark on horses to guarantee pedigree. See also *San*-branded in line 122.

6   The annually-chosen official of each of the demes or districts of Attica. He was responsible for collecting rent on land that the deme leased to individuals; he kept inventory of the property of condemned men and had the authority to enforce the surrender of securities by a debtor to a private creditor. Here the "deme official" is a bug that bites Strepsiades while he rests in his mattress.

7   A member of the important and aristocratic family of the Alcmaionids.

8   Koesyra was the mother of Megacles and Strepsiades' wife was supposedly her granddaughter. Koesyra was from Eretria, claimed to be a descendant of Zeus, and was known for her wealth and arrogance.

9   Genetyllides were goddesses of sexual intercourse and procreation and had a sanctuary at Kolias, a promontory near Phaleron where certain women's festivals which Strepsiades' wife attended were held.

10   The meaning is twofold: (1) Strepsiades' wife is extravagant; and/or (2) she is over-sexed.

11   Literally a horse, often a common prefix or suffix to proper names of men of the equestrian social class.

12   It was a common practice in ancient Athens to name male children after their paternal grandfather.

13   His name actually means "he who refrains from using horses" or "he who uses horses sparingly." But here Aristophanes uses it as a pun to indicate the opposite— Pheidippides' overindulgence in horse-racing.

14   Clasping of the right hand in greeting was considered to be an expression of friendship, good faith, trust, and affection.

15   A specialized school of novel thought, education, and customs that mainly satirizes the Sophistic Movement and the promotion of the art of speaking and oratory as a part of the new education.

16   The students of the sophists could always confuse the older, peasant population and manipulate the traditional folk with the use of dishonest argumentation.

17   Leogoras was the father of the orator Andocides, a very wealthy man who was descended from an aristocratic family connected by marriage to Pericles. One of his hobbies was raising pheasants for show (Pheidippides is equivalently mad about horses).

18   This is a specific reference to sophist Protagoras who said that "there were two arguments about every matter opposed to each other" and that there was a possibility "of making the worse argument the better."

19 Socrates' Thinking Establishment is presented as a secret society or a mystery cult where all members share certain secrets and are not permitted to divulge them to any outsiders.

20 A sort of women's shoes and a pun on the Greek word meaning flea (=*psula* is also a feminine noun).

21 The founder of the Milesian School of Natural Philosophy.

22 A very gloomy, dark place in the depths of the underworld, associated with individuals who had committed crimes of a sexual nature while they were alive (i.e. Tantalos, Sisyphos, Tityos and Ixion). Here it's used metaphorically to connect the gloominess of Socrates' Thinking School and that of mythological Hades (underworld).

23 Settlements of Athenian citizens, who were given allotments of land in territories outside Attica that had been appropriated by the Athenian state. The practice was established in late sixth century.

24 The cities of Euboea revolted from Athens in 446 BC., and the reference here is to the suppression of the revolt by the Athenian forces led by Pericles.

25 In Greek *autos*, the master or "he himself" was exclusively used by the Pythagorean philosophers and members of the cult to refer to Pythagoras himself. Here, Socrates is equated with Pythagoras as a founder of a cult. The reference here is ironic and at the same time indicates that the sophistic circles of thought were organized in the style of religious cults.

26 The study and contemplation of natural phenomena was first undertaken by the so called pre-Socratic or natural philosophers. Lines 229-234 are a distorted parody of the ideas and theories of Diogenes of Apollonia, who basically believed that the air represented the soul and mind of living creatures and, that therefore it should always be pure and dry in order that intelligent thought take place.

27 Lines 254-262 are a parody of initiation rites of a variety of mystery cults. The threefold initiation features include: (1) enthronement, (2) garlanding and (3) sprinkling with a flour substance. Aristophanes intends to show how intellectuals pursuing novel trends of thought attempted to distinguish themselves from the ordinary people by organizing into private clubs which followed the rituals and rites of the mystery cults.

28 King of Boeotia and father, with Nephele, of Phrixos and Helle. During famine, Athamas' new wife Ino misinformed the women as to how to sow seeds in order that the earth produce plentiful crops; then she told Athamas to sacrifice Phrixos in order to appease the gods and he accepted. But when he was ready to sacrifice his son, Nephele, his mother, sent a ram with golden fleece who took her children, and Phrixos was brought safe in the kingdom of Colchis. And since Athamas had listened to Ino and consented to sacrifice his son, he was himself prepared for sacrifice.

29 Patron goddess of Athens.

30 The first legendary king of Athens, thought to have been born from the earth.

31 The father of storms and winds. Also the hundred-headed monster that Zeus fought with before he established himself in the third generation of the gods and became the leader of mortals and immortals.

32 The tragic poet Hieronymos notable for the length of his hair.

33 Half-men, half-horses which were very famous for their drinking and lustfulness, making sexual advances to women and chasing nymphs in the woods to rape them.

34   A minor politician and supporter of Kleon.

35   Also a minor politician, who during the battle of Delion in 424 BC. dropped his shield and ran away.

36   A beardless effeminate Athenian satirized by comedy playwrights.

37   A distinguished sophist with various interests in the fields of religion, ethics, human psychology and the correct usage of words, contemporary with Socrates.

38   In Greek *dinos*, "rotation, whirling." It was the central concept that contributed to the development of the atomic cosmogony of Democritos and his school of scientific thought. But in everyday language *dinos* also signifies "cup." A cup statue may have stood outside Socrates' school as the statue of Hermes stood outside Strepsiades' house (*Cl.* 1473). This clearly shows the confusion of Strepsiades and it reflects on the impact that novel ideology has had upon traditional culture.

39   The most elaborate festival of Athens in honor of goddess Athena. It marked the New Year and took place on the 28th of the month *Hecatombaeon* (mid-July/mid-August). It featured parades, sacrifices, and the most extravagant meals of the year.

40   He and his wife Rhea formed the second generation of gods and were the parents of Zeus. Since Kronos is associated with the older generations of the gods, his name is used often to indicate old-fashioned, peasant-like, and even idiotic behavior.

41   An associate of the demagogue Kleon.

42   A south-eastern promontory in Athens where the temples of Poseidon and Athena stood.

43   The sacred tree of Zeus.

44   Held on the 23rd of the month *Anthesterion* (mid-February/mid-March) in honor of Zeus *Meilichios* (the kind one). There were many family celebrations with presents for the children and whole-burnt offerings.

45   The three divine groups of Socrates' Thinking Establishment are used metaphorically here to indicate that scientific speculation and the art of speaking were the only concerns of intellectualism. Thus both chaos and the clouds represent the immeasurability of natural phenomena as it was conceived in the theories of both the pre-Socratic philosophers and the sophists; while the third group, symbolized by the tongue, represents the changes in education and the cultivation of speech and oratory for courtroom purposes.

46   Trophonios had a subterranean oracular shrine at Lebadeia in Boeotia which was guarded by snakes. Therefore those visitors who descended into the shrine for consultation carried honey-cakes to appease the serpents.

47   Aristophanes speaks here in the voice of the Chorus Leader. The entire parabasis uses metaphorical language with references to Aristophanes' career, rivalries, previous work, and judgment by the Athenian judges.

48   Two brothers who were the main characters of Aristophanes' *Banqueters*. This was the poet's first comedy, and, like the *Clouds*, it dealt with the contrast between traditional and new education. Unlike the *Clouds*, however, the *Banqueters* was favored more by the judges.

49   The daughter of Agamemnon and Klytaemnestra and sister of Orestes. Major heroine for all three fifth-century tragedy playwrights in Aeschylos' *Choephoroi*, Sophocles' *Electra,* and Euripides' *Orestes*. In all three plays Orestes offers a lock of hair at his father's tomb and the lock is discovered and recognized as his by Electra. The point Aristophanes makes here is that in the same way that Electra's hope grew

when she found her brother's lock of hair, Aristophanes' own hope would grow knowing that among these spectators there are seated some intelligent men.

50   A lascivious dance associated with drunkenness.

51   In Greek *komo* means both "wear my hair long" and "give myself airs." The idiom here is a pun on Aristophanes' baldness.

52   Aristophanes had ridiculed Kleon, the most influential politician in Athens after the death of Pericles. Son of Kleaenetos, he was from Aristophanes' own deme of Cydathenaeon. Kleon died in 422, while he was leading the Athenian forces to recapture Amphipolis.

53   He was a prosecutor in the courts, entered politics in 420s and owed his wealth to a lamp-making business.

54   Another leading comedy playwright of the same generation as Aristophanes. Eupolis wrote and produced many plays and got many first prizes. In 421, his *Flatterers* defeated Aristophanes' *Peace*. He may have died in 411, during the battle of Cynossema. Maricas was the main character of Eupolis' *Maricas*, produced in 421. Maricas was a slave and paralleled the slave Paphlagon in Aristophanes' *Knights*, who was a caricature of Kleon himself.

55   Another comedy playwright contemporary of Aristophanes and Eupolis.

56   A comic dramatist of the 430s.

57   Poseidon.

58   Helios, the Sun god.

59   A nickname of Kleon, whose family's wealth depended on tanning and shoemaking business.

60   Novel ideas had an effect on the traditional calendar as regards the various festive days. Many festivals were omitted and the conventional ways of worship and ritual were giving way to skepticism and scientific speculation.

61   Memnon was king of the Ethiopians and son of Eos (Dawn), killed by Achilles during the Trojan War; Sarpedon, king of the Lycians and son of Zeus, was killed by Patroclos.

62   Measures, words and rhythms have a different meaning for Strepsiades and Socrates. To the ordinary citizen, measures are associated with capacity and not with poetic metres. Words are distinguished grammatically by genders, but Strepsiades does not know the correct usage of grammar. Finally, Socrates refers to musical rhythms of qualitative measures.

63   Socrates means the iambic trimeter (the meter of the dialogue in tragedy and comedy) and trochaic tetrameter (used mostly in comedy but also at times in tragedy).

64   In Greek *dactylos* means both "finger" and "*dactyl*=metrical foot."

65   The reference here has to do with the division of Greek nouns and adjectives into three genders: masculine, feminine, and neuter. Socrates attempts to teach Strepsiades how to correctly use all three genders in all of their cases by making him understand that there is a difference between using the noun as a subject, as direct or indirect object, vocative or to show possession.

66   A kneading tray.

67   *Koreis* in Greek is a reference to "bedbugs."

68   Strepsiades confuses intellectual thoughts with sexual and instead of producing thoughts he is busy masturbating.

69   The Thessalian witches were reputed to be able to bring the moon down.

70   This was a game played by children. A cockchafer-beetle was attached to a piece of wood too heavy for the insect to lift and was let fly at the end of a string.

71 *Pharmakos* in Greek had various meanings and applications. It could mean anything able to affect the mental or physical condition of a person who consumed it or to whom it was given as a poison, a magical charm, or a medical preparation. Glass was considered to possess such powers since it was rare, delicate, and could kindle fire. Glass was rare and precious in Greece and as important as gold.

72 The reference applies to Diagoras of Melos, who mocked all religious beliefs and practices and was condemned eventually. Strepsiades parallels and confuses Socrates with Diagoras since Socrates mocks all traditional gods and ritual too.

73 A double meaning refers to idiots and to the Titans who were born of Gaia (Earth) and were the enemies of the Olympian gods, just as the Socratics were.

74 A famous Athenian statesman. In 445 BC., when the Spartans invaded Attica, it was said that Pericles bribed the Spartan king Pleistoanax to leave with ten talents, an expense Pericles defended as for "essential purposes." Strepsiades uses the same phrase for the sake of education.

75 Jurors were paid in ancient Athens. From 423 on, jurors received three obols instead of two obols a day.

76 The two arguments allude to the dichotomy of approaches and cultural confusion that prevailed in Athens in mid-fifth century. The Just Argument stands for the ancient Greek traditional past, its conventional culture and basic educational skills, beliefs and practices. The Unjust Argument refers to the intellectual skepticism of natural philosophy and the Sophists who rejected everything that the ordinary citizens valued, trying to alter their world with their own doctrines (which mainly resulted in confusion rather than cultural enlightenment).

77 Justice (Dike) in Greek mythology dwells with the gods and traditionally sits by the side of Zeus.

78 During the battle known as Titanomachy, Zeus beat the Titans and his father Kronos and imprisoned them in the underworld. Since morality is the point here, and its ultimate fulfillment in one's respect for his parents, Zeus is deplored for his actions.

79 He was the king of Mysia (in Northwest Asia Minor south of Troy) and Aristophanes alludes to the play *Telephos* by Euripides where the king appeared disguised as a beggar. Here the reference is inverted—the Unjust Argument is disguised as a king, but in actuality he is a beggar.

80 So that they wouldn't induce self-stimulation.

81 A cithara player from the island of Lesbos who won the first prize in the Panathenaea of 456 BC.

82 It refers to their genitals.

83 There was a double standard in ancient homosexual behavior: it was considered normal for older males to be sexually attracted to younger males, but it was improper for younger males to entice older males sexually.

84 The festival of Zeus *Polieos,* celebrated on 14 *Skiraphorion* (mid-June/mid-July), was known for a very old ritual that dealt with the sacrifice of a bull, called the *Bouphonia.*

85 A very old-fashioned, contemporary dithyrambic poet.

86 Bovicide or murder of the bull was the main ritual of *Dipoleia.* The following procedure took place: various oxen were led to an altar full of grain; one ox ate the grain and was slaughtered by someone who immediately fled away; the murderer was not caught so guilt was attributed to the weapon of murder, either an axe or a knife which was purified by being thrown in the sea (salt water was purificatory);

then the ox was stuffed, raised and yoked to a plough. Since Dipoleia was a celebration preliminary to the upcoming New Year, the ritual of *Bouphonia* stood symbolically for the death of the king during the old year and the welcoming of the new elected king of the New Year, represented correspondingly by the death and symbolic resurrection of the bull.

87 An allusion to the glories of the past. The Greeks defeated the Persian forces at Marathon in 490 BC.

88 A reference to the Pyrrhic Dance in which the dancers were naked, holding their hoplite shield and performing dancing movements identical to these of a man fighting in defense and attack.

89 An epithet of Athena assigning her birth in lake Tritonis in Libya.

90 "To make a wanton display of shamelessness."

91 A Titan, brother of Kronos and father of Prometheus.

92 A nephew of Pericles, elected general for 424-425, and killed in the battle of Delion in 424. He left behind him three sons highly ridiculed in comedy: Pericles, Telesippos, and Demophon.

93 Satirized in comedy as pathic and effeminate.

94 The warm springs of Thermopylai were supposed to have been created either by Athena or Hephaestos for Heracles to wash in.

95 The king of Pylos, a very wise orator found in the *Iliad*.

96 Peleus went to the king of Iolcos, Acastos, to be purified after he killed his half brother accidently. But Acastos' wife Astydameia made sexual advances toward him. Peleus rejected her but Astydameia told Acastos that Peleus had attempted to seduce her and asked Acastos to punish Peleus. Thus Acastos took Peleus hunting but abandoned him asleep, having deprived him of his arrows. Peleus woke up surrounded by animals but Hephaestos arranged that he would be given a knife to defend himself.

97 Thetis was pursued by Zeus, but according to an oracle she was to bear a son mightier than his father. So Zeus, threatened, arranged to marry Thetis to virtuous Peleus.

98 Peleus and Thetis had a son, Achilles, mightier than his father, and Thetis decided to make him immortal by holding him over fire (fire was considered purificatory). But Peleus caught her not knowing what she was trying to do, abused her verbally in his anger and thus Thetis left him. But the Unjust Argument claims that she abandoned him because he was a lousy lover.

99 A party game associated with drunkenness and eroticism which consisted of throwing wine-lees at a target set in the midst of the diners' couches.

100 This punishment was inflicted upon an adulterer by the husband. A large rooted radish was inserted into the adulterer's *anus*, hot ash was sprinkled in his perineal region and his pubic hair was pulled out.

101 Hailstones.

102 An evil omen for the marriage since rain would extinguish the flame of the bridal torches during the procession escorting the bride to her new home.

103 The Athenians counted the days of the month after the twentieth day backwards. The last day of the month was specially called "Old-and-New." A month had either 29 or 30 days and there were 13 months in the Athenian calendar.

104 The last day of the month called as such because on the basis of the lunar calendar that the Athenians observed, it was the day when there was no moon and it stood between the old and the new month.

105 A deposit lodged in most lawsuits by both the defendant and the plaintiff with the magistrate who would supervise the case. The money would go to the state and one of the deposits would be claimed afterward by the winning party only. Thus Strepsiades would not be able to avoid a trial once a deposit was lodged against him because his opponent (the creditor) would not risk losing his deposit by withdrawing the lawsuit.

106 This refers to the payment that Strepsiades gives to Socrates for Pheidippides' educational skills. Tuition here is contrasted with the old, basic, informal education of the conventional culture.

107 Solon was *archon* in 594-593 and a renowned Athenian lawmaker to whom the people of Athens during fifth and fourth centuries attributed all laws whether he actually instituted them or not.

108 *Protenthai* (=testers) in Greek were officials who presided over the festival of *Apatouria* dealing with rites of passage celebrations. The Tasters were to test the wine and festal meal but took advantage of their position and stole the best parts.

109 A stylistically distinctive tragic dramatist of mid-fifth century, who won first prize in 446 in City Dionysia. At the outbreak of the Peloponnesian War in 431 he was one of the ten generals. He had three sons who were very famous for their dancing techniques.

110 Son of Heracles, who killed Alcmena's brother Licymnios in the tragedy *Licymnios* by Carcinos' son Xenocles.

111 A popular expression about witticism or irrationality in a person: "must have fallen off a donkey."

112 Simonides from the island of Kios (556-468) was a leading lyric poet. This is the opening line of his victory ode for a wrestler who had defeated *Krios* ("Ram") of the island of Aegina in the Nemean games:

> Sir Ram was shorn, and no wonder either,
> when he came to the splendid precinct of Zeus
> with its fine trees.

113 Pheidippides compares Strepsiades' request with a woman's work song intending to intimidate him.

114 Aeschylos was the oldest of the master tragedy playwrights of fifth century BC. Aeschylos was a very profound religious thinker and wrote mostly about the Greek past and traditional culture.

115 According to the Athenian Law, a brother and sister not born by the same mother were allowed to marry.

116 A nursery word which means "drink."

117 A nursery word which means "food."

118 An equivalent expression to English "not a fig" or "not a bean."

119 A parody of Euripides' *Alcestis* (1.691). The meaning here is: "It hurts me more than it hurts you."

120 By Greek law children owed respect to their parents, and neither father-beating nor mother-beating were acceptable. But Athenian law and custom regarded the relationship between mother and child as closer than that between father and child.

121 A cleft behind the Acropolis in Athens, into which criminals were thrown.

122 *Strepsas* in Greek derived from the verb *strephein* "twist," "turn around" and its cognates are very often used in the play with reference to Strepsiades whose name derives from the verb.

123 A cup or bowl with a rounded bottom, supported on wheels. See note 37 above.

124 The fire used here to burn the Thinking Establishment down can be interpreted variously, but the most important allusion is that fire is symbolically associated with light, the opposite of the darkness with which the play starts. Light signifies Strepsiades' realization of being fooled and at the same time alludes to a variety of oppositions within the play—for instance, the interplay between traditional culture and the novel ideas that the development of intellectualism and skepticism brought upon the simple, farmer folk.

Selected Bibliography

Adkins, A.W.H. "Some Nebulous Thoughts on the *Clouds* of Aristophanes," *Bulletin of the Institute of Classical Studies* 15 (1968)146-7
———. "*Clouds*, Mysteries, Socrates and Plato," *Antichthon* 4 (1979) 13-24
Arnott, P. *Greek Scenic Conventions in the Fifth Century BC.* (Oxford 1962)
Bowie, A.M. *Myth, Ritual and Comedy* (Cambridge 1993)
Dover, K.J. *Aristophanic Comedy* (California 1972)
Drakoulides, N.N. "Aristophanes: The *Clouds* and the *Wasps*: Foreshadowing of Psychoanalysis and Psychodrama," *American Imago* 23 (1966) 48-62
Green, P. "Strepsiades, Socrates, and the Abuse of Intellectualism," *Greek, Roman and Byzantine Studies* 20 (1978)15-25
Harriot, R.M. *Aristophanes, Poet and Dramatist* (Baltimore 1986)
Havelock, E.A. "The Socratic Self as it Is Parodied in Aristophanes' *Clouds*," *Yale Classical Studies* 22 (1972)1-18
Kopff, C.E. "*Nubes* 1493ff: Was Socrates Murdered?" *Greek, Roman and Byzantine Studies* 18 (1977)113-22
Marianetti, M.C. *Religion and Politics in Aristophanes' Clouds* (Hildesheim 1992)
McLeish, K. *The Theater of Aristophanes* (New York 1980)
O'Reagan, D. *Rhetoric, Comedy and the Violence of Language in Aristophanes' Clouds* (Oxford, 1992)
Reckford, K.J. "Aristophanes' Ever-Flowing Clouds," *Emory University Quarterly* 22 (1967) 222-35
———. *Aristophanes' Old-And-New Comedy* (Chapel Hill 1987)
Segal, C. "Aristophanes' Cloud-Chorus," *Arethusa* 2 (1969)143-51
Sifakis, G.M. *Parabasis and Animal Choruses* (London 1971)
Stone, L.M. *Costume in Aristophanic Comedy* (New York 1981)
Walcot, P. *Greek Drama in its Theatrical and Social Context* (Cardiff 1976)
Webster, T.B.L. *Greek Theatre Production* (London 1970)
Whitman, C.J. *Aristophanes and the Comic Hero* (Cambridge, Mass. 1964)
Winkler, J.J. and Zeitlin, F.I. Eds. *Nothing to Do With Dionysos? Ancient Drama in its Social Context* (Princeton 1990)